"With his graceful prose and nuanced insights, Fouad Ajami provides a magisterial account of the dramatic encounter between religious faith and state power in Saudi Arabia. From the early alliance between monarchy and Wahhabism, through the challenges of Islamist violence, to the cultural changes in the twenty-first century—especially the changing status of women—*Crosswinds* traces a narrative that testifies to the author's rich understanding of politics and intellectual history in the Kingdom and the wider Arab world as well."

—RUSSELL A. BERMAN, Walter A. Haas Professor in the Humanities, Stanford University, and senior fellow, Hoover Institution

Crosswinds
The Way of Saudi Arabia

The Hoover Institution gratefully acknowledges the following individuals and foundations for their significant support of the HERBERT AND JANE DWIGHT WORKING GROUP ON ISLAMISM AND THE INTERNATIONAL ORDER:

Herbert and Jane Dwight

Donald and Joan Beall
  Beall Family Foundation

S. D. Bechtel, Jr. Foundation

The Lynde & Harry Bradley Foundation

Nancy Doyle, MD

HERBERT AND JANE DWIGHT WORKING GROUP ON
ISLAMISM AND THE INTERNATIONAL ORDER

Crosswinds
The Way of Saudi Arabia

Fouad Ajami

HOOVER INSTITUTION PRESS
Stanford University | Stanford, California

With its eminent scholars and world-renowned library and archives, the Hoover Institution seeks to improve the human condition by advancing ideas that promote economic opportunity and prosperity, while securing and safeguarding peace for America and all mankind. The views expressed in its publications are entirely those of the authors and do not necessarily reflect the views of the staff, officers, or Board of Overseers of the Hoover Institution.

hoover.org

Hoover Institution Press Publication No. 593

Hoover Institution at Leland Stanford Junior University,
Stanford, California 94305-6003

First printing 2020
26 25 24 23 22 21 20   7 6 5 4 3 2 1

Manufactured in the United States of America
Printed on acid-free, archival-quality paper

Library of Congress Cataloging-in-Publication Data
Crosswinds : the way of Saudi Arabia / Fouad Ajami
    p. cm. — (Hoover Institution Press publication ; no. 593)
Includes bibliographical references and index.
ISBN 978-0-8179-1174-4 (cloth : alk. paper) — ISBN 978-0-8179-1176-8 (epub) — ISBN 978-0-8179-1177-5 (mobi) — ISBN 978-0-8179-1178-2 (pdf)
1. Saudi Arabia—Politics and government—1982– 2. Political culture—Saudi Arabia—History—20th century. 3. Political culture—Saudi Arabia—History—21st century. 4. Saudi Arabia—Foreign relations—1982–
I. Herbert and Jane Dwight Working Group on Islamism and the International Order. II. Title.
DS244.63.A37 2020
953.805'3—dc22   2010030942

For Megan Ring,
a partner and friend who made so much possible
with heart and humor and intellect

Contents

Foreword

From his philosopher's study in a Baltic seaport, Immanuel Kant took on the intellectual problem of promoting peace in the world. This was the kind of thing Enlightenment thinkers did; Kant's project would emerge as a structure for the modern international state system.

Kant's logic chain began with the extreme places of the world. Arabia, as Fouad Ajami's masterwork *Crosswinds* never lets us forget, is the *extrême de la extrême*: in climate, topography, faith, and fanaticism. Ever since the swift, stunning rise of Islam, most intensively through the Victorian nineteenth and war-riven twentieth centuries, "orientalist" scholars and aesthetes, adventurous travelers in disguise on the hajj, sojourners, diplomats, journalists, and spies tried to grasp this phenomenon. Some were alarmed by what they found, others intrigued, many captivated by "heart-beguiling Araby." In our time, as the stakes grew ever higher, a cadre of policy and security analysts urgently joined the search for clues to the riddle of the sands.

At last we have Fouad Ajami, a uniquely gifted figure in this cavalcade, a thinker and a writer of astounding insight and depth: Muslim, scholar, political philosopher, category-defying public intellectual, American—just the one Kant must have hoped would arrive to carry his logic chain forward.

Put most simply, Kant concluded that the cause of peace would most pragmatically be advanced through an international association of states with republican governance and the willingness to refrain from bringing their religious beliefs to the negotiating table of world affairs and to foster an open trading system that would benefit, and benefit from, those extreme regions of the world. Thus we see the immense significance of today's Saudi Arabia, whose statehood has been indispensable but profoundly troubled, whose religious faith has been internationally hyperactive, and whose world trade has been dominated by the "curse" of oil.

Ajami makes good use of his predecessors, the Victorian travelers Palgrave and Hogarth, but not until the final page does he mention Doughty, the best of them all.

Travels in Arabia Deserta, published in 1888 by Charles Montagu Doughty, gained a reputation as a monumental achievement of English prose. In it Doughty created an elevated, archaic style to convey the elaborately wild yet elegant culture of honor and blood of the Arab tribes. The book was, as its student T. E. Lawrence (of Arabia) wrote, "the first and indispensable work upon the Arabs." Lawrence summed it up: The Arabs have "no half-tones in their register of vision." They show no longing for great industry; "their largest manufacture [is] of creeds." Their thoughts live easiest among extremes, the only refuge and rhythm of their being is in God. He is "the commonest of their thoughts." The Arabs Doughty dwelt among were unselfconscious in their premodern authenticity, as yet undeparted from what twentieth-century philosophers would call their "being."

But, noted Lawrence, writing after World War I, during the decades after Doughty wrote *Arabia Deserta*, the Arabs "had learned enough of the ideas of Europe to accept nationality as a basis for action. They accepted it so thoroughly that they went into battle against their Caliph, the Sultan of Turkey, to win their right to national freedom." Out of this idea would come Saudi Arabia as a state in the international state system.

Herein dwells the dilemma of Saudi Arabia today. By the self-assessment of the Saudi hierarchy, ensconced upon the three pillars of tribal authenticity, royal supremacy, and religious orthodoxy, no regime, no polity conceivably could be more Muslim than they. The Saudi flag says it all: a field of green representing the faith with the calligraphic creed "There is no God but Allah, and Mohammed is his Prophet," underlined by the sword of strength and conviction.

Imagine then the shock as Ajami vividly describes what happened in November 1979, coincident with the fourteenth century of the Islamic calendar, when fanatics, proclaiming the arrival of the Mahdi, the redeemer, seized control of the sanctuary and mosque of the Kaaba in Mecca—Islam's most sacred site. Saudi Arabia, self-defined as impeccably Islamic yet also as a legitimate sovereign state, faced the radical charge that the two—Islam and the state—are incompatible. From this point forward the Saudis would try to ride both galloping steeds at the same time: statehood in a global economy and an ever more radical Wahhabi observance of the faith. Saudi Arabia thus stands for what may be seen as a momentous civil war within the Muslim Middle East: those who seek to be both authentically Muslim and internationally responsible versus those who say Islam cannot tolerate the established world order and must oppose and replace it.

In the lands of the Middle East today, Iran no longer presents to the true believers the inspirational model and the challenge it did in 1979. Yet the Saudi monarchy must still, in some way, balance reform and a pro-Western orientation with the traditions and beliefs that run deep in segments of that society, and the pride and sense of exceptionalism that color the way Saudis face the world. It is Ajami's unique access to all levels of Saudi society that gives this work its depth and clarity.

Ajami's book is no traveler's account but a work of profound political thought, bringing world-historical complexities into the lives of Arabs high and low to illuminate their tensions and hopes as no other writer could do. *Crosswinds* is thus a classic for our time, worthy of mention in the same sentence with Doughty's great volume, and might well have been titled *Arabia Perplexa*.

I have at hand the battered copy of the *Oxford Book of English Prose* chosen by the Victorian-era don Sir Arthur Quiller-Couch, which forty years ago accompanied me to Vietnam. Mine is the 1925 edition; there hasn't been one since, an indicator of the parlous state of the literary art. Doughty's *Arabia Deserta* is represented here. If an edition for our time were possible, surely Ajami's prose would be featured. This is more than a matter of style. The greatest prose masters possess intellectual, emotional, and visual intelligence all at once; they see the universe at a unique angle of vision, and their human and societal portraits exfoliate beyond metaphor into vocabularies and cadences of matchless instructional value. In *Crosswinds*, as in Fouad Ajami's entire oeuvre, we see the ideas, emotions, and objects of Arabia as, in Doughty's words, "a flowering tree full of murmuring bees of the desert."

CHARLES HILL
Research Fellow, Hoover Institution
Cochairman, Herbert and Jane Dwight Working Group
on Islamism and the International Order

Preface

The most sustained American inquiry into the trail of Islamist radicalism, the 9/11 Commission Report, could not really crack the Saudi riddle. The commissioners and their staff had given the terror of September 11, 2001, their most concentrated official assessment. After the public hearings and after the expert testimonies, the report noted the opaqueness of the Saudi realm, the ambivalence that ran through its tangled relationship with its American protector: "Saudi Arabia has been a problematic ally in combating Islamic extremism. At the level of high policy, Saudi Arabia's leaders cooperated with American diplomatic initiatives aimed at the Taliban or Pakistan before 9/11. At the same time, Saudi Arabia's society was a place where Al Qaeda raised money directly from individuals and through charities. It was the society that produced 15 of the 19 hijackers." The oil-for-protection bargain had broken down: a relationship that had been an affair of the two governments was now in full public view. And the relationship could not stand up to scrutiny. America had been in Arabia for well over six decades; yet the American access to the inner workings of the Saudi world was limited at best. The 9/11 Commission could only scratch the surface of things. The Americans had not really known that "problematic ally."

What follows is an attempt to fill a gap in our understanding of that country. There are travel notes, but they are not definitive, for this is not a traveler's account. I am lucky to have some access, gained over the course of two decades, to Saudis drawn from a broad segment of the population. I try in these pages to be true to what they told me. I have dispensed with their names, for this is an overly discreet country, and there is nothing to be gained from providing these names.

Luck came my way in the sudden emergence of a new wave of Saudi literature, works of fiction and biography that afford us a new view of the Saudi reality. A generation earlier, that country was relatively silent. But Saudis are now writing revealing literary works, and I have drawn on a fair amount of this new literature. The bulk of it is unavailable in English, and it was immensely rewarding to try to do justice to it. Then there are the bloggers, their verve and irreverence, and the immediacy of what they write, providing a window onto the world of the skeptics and the modernists in that land.

Once upon a time, Saudis were consumers of the literature of Beirut and Cairo and Damascus. Now they render their own world. To be sure, they are not free in the Beiruti way, or in the way of the Arab diaspora in Europe, but they can now be heard and read. I don't ask in these pages the sort of questions that have been the norm in the standard writing on Arabia— the sources of instability, the prospects of its rulers, the problems of succession from one royal to another. I try to depict the journey of that country from the early 1990s to the present day. In the 1990s, it was the practice to write of a crisis of the regime—some wrote its obituary. But the order rode out that storm. The religious diehards did not carry the day. But they have fed a current of obscurantism and a culture of intolerance toward "the other" that haunts their country. There is a price, too, that countries pay for stability.

These pages walk a fine line between the political culture of Saudi Arabia and its conduct and influence in foreign lands. I have not drawn a sharp distinction; my aim was to chart the Saudi way both at home and abroad. An inquiry into the political culture of Saudi Arabia is, by necessity, an inquiry into the matter of Islam in its public life. My working assumption is simple: men and women cut all religious cloth to their preference, they make of religion what they are inclined toward. Something the great American novelist Cormac McCarthy wrote in his stunning work *The Road* informs my view. "Where men can't live gods fare no better," he observed. Religion is there, and the believers work their will on it. They endow it with mercy or with unforgiving zeal, it can shelter or it can forbid and scold.

The dominant creed in Saudi Arabia is the Wahhabi doctrine—though strictly speaking, Saudis frown on that designation, for to them their faith is the pristine message of Islam itself, unsullied by heresies and deviations. The mind of Wahhabism, and its workings, will become clearer in the pages that follow. But this much can be said by way of precision and background. Wahhabism is named for a stern influential jurist of Central Arabia, Muhammad ibn Abdul Wahhab (1703–92). This desert preacher cast himself in the role of a reformer and a "purifier" of Islam from the "compromises" and accretions

that befell it since its rise. The principle of *tauhid* (the assertion of the divine unity of God) is central to Wahhabi thought.
The founder of this creed was given to a belief that Islam had
been disfigured by doctrines of mysticism, by the visitation of
shrines, by the kinds of beliefs the minority sects of Islam—the
Shi'a, in the main, but other sects as well—brought into Islam. It
was Muhammad ibn Abdul Wahhab who struck the deal, in the
mid-eighteenth century, that still anchors the Saudi state: the
alliance between the religious scholars, the *ulama*, who adhere
to Wahhabism's exacting and severe teachings, and the House
of Saud.

FOUAD AJAMI
Stanford, California, 2010

Acknowledgments

I have incurred many debts along the way. Countless Saudi friends were incomparable in their kindness to me, their hospitality worthy of all that has been said and written about Arab hospitality. Their culture is one of discretion, so I have not named them. My hope is that, were they to read this work, they would find in it a worthwhile depiction of their world.

Professor Charles Doran, my colleague at the Paul H. Nitze School of Advanced International Studies (SAIS) at Johns Hopkins University, gave me encouragement to press on with this book when I needed it. My younger SAIS colleague, Professor Camille Pecastaing, is an exacting scholar. I am grateful to him for his insistence that earlier drafts still needed more of the texture of the Saudi realm.

At the Hoover Institution, I was lucky for the friendship and support of Charles Hill and John Raisian. Charlie, "the man on whom nothing was lost," took time out of working on his thrilling work, *Grand Strategies*, to read mine. John Raisian was all academics dream of in the way of deans and directors but rarely get. He conceived the project out of which this book grew, gave it sustenance, and carried it along and made room for me at

Hoover. He and his colleagues, and the good people at Hoover Institution Press, are consummate professionals. I am particularly grateful to Jennifer Presley, Marshall Blanchard, Jennifer Navarrette, and Denise Elson for their commitment in getting this book to press. And to the cause of Hoover and its work.

As in two earlier longer books, and scores of essays and reviews, I couldn't have done this without my assistant, colleague, and friend at SAIS, then at Hoover, Megan Ring. Megan, as is known to one and all I know in Arabia, Baghdad, and elsewhere, can do many things at the same time. For her friendship, for her faith in this project, I am truly in her debt. As is her way, Michelle Ajami would rather not be thanked, but this work, too, bears her mark. At SAIS, Katarina Lesandric, who administers the Middle East program, was helpful and supportive in many ways.

Secretary George P. Shultz took time out of an impossibly busy schedule to give this text a sustained and critical reading. I am grateful to him for his kindness and for his interest in my work. The Middle East was but one arena to which George Shultz applied his formidable talents of diplomacy and statecraft. The world of that Greater Middle East has always tugged at him. It is in this spirit that the text could be read as an attempt to answer the sort of questions that engaged him in his years in office and in the years hence.

FOUAD AJAMI
Stanford, California, 2010

In the ten years since this book was completed for publication, much has changed in Saudi Arabia—and not changed. Fouad had no inkling of the rise of Mohammed bin Salman, but there was much he sought to understand on a deeper level. It was a society that profoundly intrigued him—"the magic kingdom," as he liked to say—a realm obscured to outsiders, more than other Middle Eastern lands, by layers of custom and profound discretion. There is a great deal in his reading of the place that peels away those layers and helps set in context the events of today.

We had long grappled with the desire to put this to press, and it was Dr. Cole Bunzel who ultimately gave it the nod towards the light. As a student who was held in highest regard by Fouad, his enthusiasm for this project was decisive. The new introduction he has provided grounds this work in the present. For this and for his careful reading and editing, we are both enormously grateful. Fouad would have been proud to have his final touches on this manuscript.

Barbara Arellano gave her wholehearted support—once again—to publication and pulled out all the stops to make it happen in a timely way. Danica Michels Hodge and Alison Law lent their formidable talents in the most gracious and effective way, sensitive to all Fouad's predilections as if he'd been there to oversee the project. Denise Elson has been a vital and key part of everything Fouad did at Hoover. She never hesitated for a moment in reviving this book. She, Chris Dauer, and Shana Farley were always the team Fouad turned to.

Charlie Hill and Russell Berman, with Fouad, were the pillars that conceived and breathed life into the working group that produced a stellar lineup of publications, of which this was one. They have been true to that original concept and mission ever since. Eric Wakin, the inimitable head of the Hoover Library & Archives, has been caretaker of all Fouad's papers, and his constant support has been reassuring and inspiring.

Finally, we want to add a special word of thanks to Miriam Sofaer—and her husband, Abe—for the fundamental role they played.

MICHELLE AJAMI AND MEGAN RING
Stanford, California, 2020

Introduction

The publication of *Crosswinds: The Way of Saudi Arabia* has been a long time coming. Fouad Ajami's intimate portrait of Saudi society and politics, drawing on his visits to the kingdom in the 1990s and early 2000s, was finished in 2010. The manuscript was submitted to Hoover Institution Press that year, and in the coming months it would be edited and typeset. But before its release Ajami put the book on hold, partly out of concern for the security of some of the Saudi sources identified, though never named, in the text. Unfortunately, what started as a temporary pause turned into an interminable delay as new developments in the Middle East beckoned.

In late 2010, a revolution took place in Tunisia, and soon a revolutionary fervor swept the region. The Arab Spring, as it would be called, seemed to usher in a new era in Arab politics. Regimes were toppled as crowds called for freedom and dignity and an end to oppression. Ajami was enthusiastic about this moment, hopeful that the Arab world might finally overcome the endemic corruption and tyranny that had plagued it for decades. During this time, I was his student at the Johns Hopkins

School of Advanced International Studies in Washington—the last year he taught, 2010–11. "The Egyptians have surprised the hell out of me," he said in class of the uprising in Egypt that followed hard on Tunisia's. "My enthusiasm for the revolt in Egypt is boundless." In February 2011, when President Hosni Mubarak of Egypt was finally deposed, he brought champagne to class.

The next great battleground in the revolutionary upheaval was in Syria. Peaceful protests broke out in early 2011 and soon gave way to a full-fledged civil war. In 2012 Ajami published a book on the conflict, *The Syrian Rebellion*, charting the uprising's course. "Of the Arab societies stirred by the turmoil of 2010–2011," he wrote, "Syria stands alone in the price paid by its peoples, and the cruelty and tenacity of the regime." Indeed, exceptional circumstances had led him to Syria. He had put the Saudi book aside.

For better or worse, the Arab Spring did not visit Saudi Arabia. Ajami was not surprised. "This realm is not fragile," he once remarked in class. The Saudis were in fact the counter-revolutionary power. They intervened to prevent an uprising in neighboring Bahrain and gave refuge to the deposed Tunisian president, Zine El Abidine Ben Ali, who died in Jeddah in 2019.

In June 2014, Fouad Ajami died, far too early, after a short battle with cancer. He would never have the opportunity to return to the Saudi book. Surely he would have liked to revise and update it substantially before seeing it published, but there is no use in sitting on the manuscript forever. Enough time has passed to allay his earlier concerns. It is a small tribute to him that Hoover Institution Press has agreed, with the support of Michelle Ajami, to bring out *Crosswinds* in its original form.

Much of course has changed in the kingdom since 2010. The long reign of King Abdullah, who ruled effectively from 1995 onward, came to an end with his death in 2015. He was succeeded by his half-brother Salman, one of the last surviving sons of the founder of the modern kingdom. In practice it has been Salman's favored son, Mohammed bin Salman—known by his initials, MbS—who has managed the daily affairs of state. In 2017, MbS assumed the role of Crown Prince, thus making him the heir apparent. His ascension, whenever it takes place, will mark the first generational change in the leadership of Saudi Arabia since 1953, the year when King Abd al-Aziz Ibn Saud, the founder of the modern kingdom, died.

The rise of MbS heralds a new era in Saudi history, one possessed of both promise and peril. On the one hand the Crown Prince has overseen an unprecedented series of social and economic reforms, intended to make Saudi Arabia into a more "normal" country. He has opened the country to tourism, stripped the religious police of their power of arrest, granted women the right to drive, legalized movie theaters and concerts, and eliminated public flogging as a punishment. He has sought to encourage foreign investment and cultivate the non-oil sector of the economy. As regards the U.S.-Saudi security relationship, he has shown less regard for the idea of keeping the United States at a distance, inviting U.S. military forces to return to the kingdom after a nearly seventeen-year absence. Through much of this he has dramatically curtailed the power and influence of the religious establishment, the historical partner of the House of Saud in running the country. Indeed, MbS has played down the formative role of the Saudi version of Islam, known as Wahhabism, in the history of the kingdom.

At the same time, Saudi Arabia under MbS has become a more repressive and authoritarian country. In an essay from the early 1990s, Ajami described Saudi Arabia and the other Gulf monarchies as "a benign political order": "No 'visitors of dawn' haul people off to political prisons in the dynastic states; men do not 'disappear' as they do in Damascus and Baghdad." MbS has done much to challenge that description. No dissent to his policies is tolerated. All sorts of alleged dissidents, from religious actors to liberal reformers, have been rounded up and detained. Many of these, such as female advocates of women's driving, pose no discernible threat to his rule. Then there was the incident in October 2018 that sparked international outrage. At the Saudi consulate in Istanbul, Saudi agents brutally murdered the journalist and commentator Jamal Khashoggi, possibly as part of an attempt to repatriate him by force. Khashoggi had sought refuge in the United States, where he wrote critically of the Crown Prince, speaking in one article of the "climate of fear and intimidation" that had descended on the kingdom.

MbS, it is fair to say, does not fully adhere to "the way of Saudi Arabia" that forms the subject of this book. The Saudi way was a cautious one: halting reforms, benign authoritarianism, deference to the religious establishment, and royal consensus. In this last regard MbS has again departed from precedent.

Traditionally, Saudi kings were, as Ajami put it in a late 2010 commentary, "first among equals" with their brothers: "The sons of Ibn Saud have had a way of dividing the power and the spoils of their father's inheritance." Today such royal power-sharing is no longer practiced. MbS has moved aggressively to concentrate power in himself at the expense of his relatives, stripping many of their portfolios and assets and reportedly placing some under house arrest.

Given the changes in Saudi Arabia over the past five years, *Crosswinds* may appear dated in some respects. It does well, however, in putting current developments into perspective. Focusing on the 1990s and the first decade of the 2000s, the book covers the critical events of the Gulf War, 9/11, the Al Qaeda revolt of 2003–6, and the U.S. intervention in Iraq from the Saudi perspective. In addition to his travels in the kingdom, Ajami draws on his extensive and varied reading—newspapers, *fatwa*s, memoirs, travelogues, and novels—in depicting the "Saudi way" that was the hallmark of this period. The book, to borrow a phrase from the late L. Carl Brown, is "vintage Ajami." It "crisply presents characters and anecdotes, using them as springboards for musings on larger issues." Many of its recurring themes still bear much relevance to the current situation in the kingdom—the balance between reform and tradition, the strength and resilience of the political order, the problem of jihadism at home and abroad.

While *Crosswinds* does not predict or anticipate what has happened in Saudi Arabia during the last five years, its author rightly understood that "the personal factor matters in a monarchy of this sort." For this reason, he was uncertain about the future of the country. There was, in the words of one of his Saudi interlocutors, a "silent crisis in the land," a certain dissatisfaction and despair felt by many segments of society. MbS has sought to alleviate this crisis. Whether he can succeed without provoking another remains to be seen.

COLE BUNZEL
Hoover Fellow, Hoover Institution
Stanford, California, 2020

CHAPTER ONE

Prologue:
The Chastening

"Not much has changed since you were here last, has it?" a young worldly businessman in Jeddah whom I had known for more than two decades said to me in the summer of 2009. I had been in and out of Saudi Arabia throughout the 1990s. I had made, as my text will make clear, a difficult trip in 2002, a time when emotions—mine and my hosts'—were raw, so close were we to the terror attacks of 9/11. In the years that followed, Iraq had fully engaged me and my concern with Saudi Arabia was secondary; what I looked for, from afar, was the Saudi response to Iraq. My return to Saudi Arabia was an attempt to understand what had taken place within the Saudi realm. My host had warmly welcomed me back. He opened his family's home for me—the grace and hospitality of people there redeem the country and are at such variance with the stern exterior of the place. I understood what he meant and why he said what he said, but an outsider could see and sense that things had altered there.

Seven years earlier, there had been endless laments that Saudis didn't have the ruler they needed. Many repeatedly spoke with sorrow and nostalgia of the late King Faisal (ruled

1964–75). He had been the last "real monarch," they said of him. He had been an immensely disciplined man, he had moved his country forward while keeping the religious establishment in check. By standards of Arabia and the Gulf, he had been austere—no monumental palaces, no extravagant spending. In the telling, he had negotiated the Saudi-American relationship while keeping faith with wider Arab and Islamic loyalties. There had been drift in the years of the two men who came after him, Khalid and Fahd. A great deal of ground had been ceded to the religious establishment, more broadly to the religious reactionaries. The access of the royals to the public treasure had grown brazen, and it was during those years that the Hijazis in the more religiously tolerant western part of the country had lost ground to the kingdom's heartland in Najd. The money and the royal favor and patronage had shifted to the more religiously and culturally severe Najdis. The Najdi version of Islam had triumphed. There had been no Hijazi *imam* of the Grand Mosque in years, and this sat uneasily with the Hijazis; they had no prominent members in the high ranks of the judiciary or the senior *ulama,* the community of scholars.

I had returned four years into King Abdullah's reign. Was this what the modernists had been hoping for? I spoke with a technocrat in his early forties in the Eastern Province, a man who had never been taken in by the official version of things and who had traveled widely and lived abroad for a good number of years; he said that this monarch would decisively win a free election. He had opened a national dialogue and showed every indication that he understood the desire for change; he had been more supportive of women's rights—an influential and outspoken daughter of his had emerged as a leader in women's causes. He had reined in the extravagance. He accepted that the country's educational system was a colossal failure, and had appointed a son-in-law, schooled at Stanford University, as minister of education. More novel and daring still, he had selected a woman with a graduate degree from Utah State University as deputy minister of education. The repair had begun, this young technocrat said. There were no guarantees of success, but grant this ruler the credit for giving it a try.

A more unsentimental interpretation was given to me by a disaffected academic, fifty years of age. The king was impulsive and blunt, he said, suspicious in the way of Bedouin culture. Saudis recognized more of themselves in him, they spoke of him with both reverence and familiarity, he added, referred to him as Abu (father of) Miteeb, after his oldest son. He didn't put on airs, he spoke bluntly to foreign leaders, and he put American officials on notice that Arabia would make its own calls on vital matters of security and regional concerns. But I was not to exaggerate what King Abdullah can do, or how deeply he sees into the heart of matters, I was warned. The monarch was in his eighties, his skills were tactical, his education rather limited. He did not have the wider horizons of Faisal or the administrative skills of Fahd. Kingship came to him, but the ability to transform the country, repair its educational system, move its sluggish bureaucracy, was beyond him. He had his half-brothers, and though he was the first among equals, the senior princes could still thwart any reformist project.

When the king designated Minister of Interior Prince Naif second deputy prime minister, the reformists drew back. The dour prince, so close to the religious establishment and a patron of the *mutawwa* (religious police), had been given a clear shot at succession. No other senior member of the royal family is viewed with the unease that the liberals have for Naif. The state was a *salafi* state (one that strictly follows tradition), Naif believed; he was not one to play to liberal sentiment or to court popularity and approval. He was the quintessential autocrat: he beheld the world beyond Arabia's borders with unadorned suspicion. He has been a forceful advocate of the view that it was idle to discuss the issue of women's rights. For all the talk of an "allegiance council" that would open up the succession to a discussion within the royal clan, Abdullah had given in to the weight of custom and to the prerogatives of *al-thaluth*, the triangle—his three Sudairi half-brothers (related to the Sudairi clan through their mother): Crown Prince Sultan, Minister of Interior Naif, and the influential governor of Najd, Prince Salman.

The stranger's luck: it brought my way two talented men of public affairs, one in Jeddah, the other in the Eastern Province. They had a gift of narrative and a willingness to look into their country's troubles. I didn't have to explain much; they knew what I was after, they were willing to cut into the tangle of concerns that had brought me to Arabia.

"The religious radicals are in retreat, they've lost the monopoly they once had on religious subjects, religious knowledge is easily available, 'Shaykh Google' is now the most influential source of knowledge," the man from Jeddah, a journalist in his mid-forties, bright and inquisitive and self-possessed, said to me.

The bloggers are multiplying by the day, people have access to knowledge, they can dial a *fatwa* on any subject of choice, this is not the same society it was a decade or so earlier. I remember when a neighbor of ours was the first to have cable news. We were glued to CNN, that neighbor had an honored and prestigious place; now satellite dishes are everywhere, the Chinese-made dishes are sold for a pittance. There is no need to defer to any particular religious preacher, for *fatwas* and opinions can be easily found. Saudi society is plenty religious at any rate. Peddling piety to Saudis is like trying to sell water in a water-sellers' market. The extremists are no match for the state. The radical preachers who came into fame and influence in the 1990s have moved on. Their most prominent figure, Safar al-Hawali, has suffered a stroke; Salman al-Awda and Ayid al-Qarni have gone mainstream, and have become pop stars. This is what they wanted all along—they used to preach before a handful of people, now they have vast television audiences.

He reached for an American analogy and he found it: "These preachers are now part Dear Abby, offering advice to the bewildered, and part Rick Warren, the popular California preacher." The state lets these men be, he said, for it has nothing to fear from them.

I had been told that this man had had a brush or two with the authorities, that he had reached his own accommodation with the ruling order. He was no sycophant, he had high pedigree, a knack for political and economic analysis, and a place in the media. All wasn't well, he said, the limits on free expression cripple the public space, but to him the religious extremists were cultists: "Saudis discovered that the extremists have nothing to offer." He echoed the wider verdict that once the extremists took up arms against the state they were doomed. The space for liberty was small, he conceded. He gave the rulers their due—they were shrewd in the ways of power. He had to his judgment a tone of resignation. The country was what it was, he did not think that it would attempt any great breakthroughs. He was a Hijazi, but he took in stride the decline of the Hijazis relative to Najd. The Hijazis are loners, he said, they can't work together, they were not ready for the energy of the Najdis and their sense of solidarity.

In the Eastern Province, I was offered a less resigned view of things. This was odd and unexpected, for it came from a Shi'a political analyst and information entrepreneur, fifty years old. A lunch had been given for me in the home of a technocrat in Dhahran. Intended or not, it was a Shi'a gathering, a simple affair, a group of five noted professionals from this region. The house was airy, the unpretentious home of a professional, a small garden outside, the furniture in good, simple taste. Children walked in, polite and well dressed, it was a Friday (the Muslim day of worship and thus a day off from school), and they were welcomed and fussed over.

I had cheated myself, I had talked more than I should have. They were keen to know of Iraq and of Lebanon, they wanted to know what the presidency of Barack Obama offered for the region. There was a quiet presence in the room, that of the man who identified himself as a "political development analyst." There was an unbent quality to him. It had been a free-for-all discussion, he had kept his interventions to a minimum, and I had decided I would seek a narrative from him about his

province, about the Shi'a, and about the wider "political development" of the realm.

I wouldn't be disappointed. He gave me the entire next day,
picked me up from the Holiday Inn, by the highway, where I
was staying. (A special debt is owed the host who rescues a
stranger from the hotel lobbies of a country with a forbidding
public space.) He took me to the town of Qatif—the principal
Shi'a town—and gave me entry to this place that I had come
for. He had a PhD from England, he had spent long years in
exile—in Iran, Kuwait, and, of course, England. People here
shy away from political discussions; he savored them. I never
asked if he had spent time in prison, but I know he had begun
his Shi'a activism as a very young man, at the height of the enthusiasm—and panic—generated by the Iranian Revolution, that
he had left the country only to return in 1994, when an uneasy
accommodation had been reached between the government
and the Shi'a oppositionists. By then, the ideological appeal of
the Iranian Revolution had faded, and the House of Saud had
decided to live and let live with its Shi'a critics. (That reckoning
had come, in no small measure, because of the neo-Wahhabi
unrest in Najd; the rulers had concluded that the Shi'a in the
Eastern Province were no threat to the realm.)

What adversity this man knew hadn't dented his innate
optimism. "A sophisticated political society is putting down
roots," he said.

> We have forty-two private television channels—they are not
> legal, but the state has stepped out of the way, in a kind of
> "don't ask, don't tell" accommodation. We have more than
> three hundred nongovernmental associations, they are

neither banned nor licensed. The society goes its own way, it has outgrown the rulers' will and the rulers' control. We have political parties in all but name. There is our movement, the Shi'a-based Reform Movement; there is Salman al-Awda in Najd, he has his own movement, Najdi-based neo-Wahhabis, that draws its adherents from the Najdi middle class and its money from the rich bankers in Riyadh; there are liberal constitutionalists drawn from the ranks of the professionals; there is a Hezbollah movement in the Eastern Province.

No one is waiting on the royals, it is enough that they know their limits and we know ours. King Abdullah has opened greater space for reform, but he can't control the floodgates. We met with him several times, my colleagues and myself in the Reform Movement, when he was Crown Prince. He signaled that he understood our demands for equality and for redress of grievances, but we have not had access to him during his kingship. In all fairness, we understand that Shaykh Salman al-Awda, too, had not been able to see him. As a Shi'a I know I am oppressed, I know the limits of this society. I can't transcend my Shi'ism, neither wealth nor education would enable me to go beyond my Shi'ism. I accept this, but I don't want to be discriminated against in a blatant way. We are of this land, and this country. There had been a ban on travel to Iran, it was lifted in 1995–96, and those who went to Iran returned disillusioned with that experiment. It was not the promised land, they discovered. They saw poverty in Iran, the shelves in the stores were empty, there was more religious orthodoxy than they expected, they were now more appreciative of what they had in their own country.

No one here wants to overturn the order, they want it reformed and modernized, made more tolerant. We want basic rights, we can't build Shi'a mosques, so when one of our clerics led the prayer in the basement of his own house, he was arrested. We have little if any contact with the provincial government. Prince Mohamed bin Fahd has been governor for more than two decades, we barely know him, but that's not unusual, he keeps to himself and to his circle of retainers. We had had a privileged role in the oil industry, we had the skills for it because government employment had not been available for us, but now there are greater limits on us in the oil industry. Sensitive jobs in refining, in oil security, are denied us.

"There is an appetite for greater freedom," he insisted. I had led him there by suggesting that the place had no yearning for liberty, that it preferred the security of what it knew.

Go to the causeway that connects us to Bahrain on the eve of our weekly break. It is choked with traffic. We have everything Bahrain has, only cheaper. We have parts of the country, by the mountains around Taif, which are as beautiful as Lebanon. Yet five to six million Saudis travel abroad every year—to Bahrain, to Lebanon, to Egypt, to European destinations—in search of greater personal freedom. Once they step on foreign soil, they dispense with the shackles that limit them here. Their children see this schizophrenia in their elders' lives; this kind of restrictive order lives on borrowed time. We have eighty thousand students abroad now, twenty-six thousand of them in the United States, fourteen thousand of them in Britain. They will want more than economic security, they will want a modern life. There is an innate Saudi appetite for "new" things—fast food, satellite dishes, cell phones, all the gadgets. Admittedly, this is not political freedom, but the old ways are destined to fall.

We spent a day around Qatif. Little relieved the eye. It was summer, and the heat was fierce. The waters of the Gulf were green and rancid, and still. The trees and the shrubs planted by the highway were a reminder that everything here has to be secured against an unforgiving physical harshness. It was a veritable moonscape, and it raised for me, as it always does when I am there, thoughts of the rulers' advantage: they keep the place going, they plant the shrubs, there is no merciful public space— no shade—where their opponents could meet. "There are the mosques and the malls," a young friend reminded me, a way of acknowledging the limits of public life in this country. A senior member of the royal family is said to bluntly assert in his private councils that the House of Saud conquered the Peninsula by the sword, and that those who want to take their domain from them better be prepared to claim it by the sword as well. Few Saudis today believe that the realm is up for grabs.

Those things more fundamental than royal succession, more than the comings and goings of the royals and the gossip about their personal fortunes, were underlined for me by a retired technocrat in Dhahran, seventy years of age, Shi'a but married to an exquisitely cultured Sunni wife.

> Here in the Eastern Province we used to be the breadbasket of the Peninsula, we grew rice of the highest quality, and this is now of the past. Go find a Saudi tailor, we did exquisite embroidery work. Now the stitchers are gone, they married Syrian women and made their way there. The stitching is done by Indians and Pakistanis. We wear what we don't make, we eat what we don't grow. We can easily conjure up

the expatriates leaving us one day. On that day we would find ourselves without skills, without proper education. You are told that we beat back the extremists, the terrorists. But this doesn't matter, they don't need weapons. They have power over our destiny, over the kind of schooling we can have, they have a stranglehold on the culture. Look at our appalling educational system. There is talk of building magnificent libraries, there is in the works a university for science and technology. But there is no free inquiry, we don't have the rudiments of a scientific culture. We have religious scholars with prestige and standing obsessing over sorcery and witchcraft. A number of them firmly believe that volcanoes and earthquakes are not phenomena of the natural world but acts of divine will meant as a rebuke to God's creatures who stray from the proper path. We have a belligerent religious ideology, our young people go to the mosques and the prayer leaders ask the Almighty to make widows of infidel women, orphans of infidel children. Oil sustains all this, devours the alternatives. This is the ride we have taken, it doesn't truly matter which member of the royal family gains the upper hand. Think of us in the Eastern Province, we're for all practical purposes an occupied country. The rulers are from Najd, the mentality is Najdi to the core, and there is little we can do about it.

The man grieved for a lost age and a spoilt garden. In a chronicle of the 1860s, a classic of desert writing by William Gifford Palgrave, *Personal Narrative of a Year's Journey through Central and Eastern Arabia (1862–63)*, I found the same lament, a traveler's vision of what was once there and what was to come. Palgrave had come to Hasa, this eastern part of the Peninsula, from Najd. He came with an aversion to the Wahhabis of Central Arabia, and he was to feel an affinity for this worldly people on the Persian Gulf—cultivators and merchants, "a sea-coast people looking mainly to foreign lands and the ocean for livelihood and commerce, accustomed to seeing among them not infrequently men of dress, manners, and religion differing from their own." The stitchers of my host's imagination turned up in Palgrave's rendition:

> For centuries Hasa had carried on a flourishing commerce with Oman, Persia, and India on the right, and with Basra and Baghdad on the left, nay even with Damascus itself, in spite of political hostility and local distance. For the cloaks of Hasa manufacture, and the embroidery which adorns them, are alike unrivalled; such delicacy of work, such elegance of pattern, are unknown save in Cachemire [Kashmir] alone. The wool employed is of exquisite fineness, and, when skillfully interwoven with silk, forms a tissue alike strong to wear and beautiful to the eye; while its borderings of gold and silver thread, tastefully intermixed with the gayest colours, may be envied but never equaled, by Syria and Persia.

There had been bliss and prosperity, Palgrave writes, but "now all is fallen away; the Nejdean eats out the marrow and the fat of the land; while his senseless war against whatever it pleases his fanaticism to proscribe under the name of luxury— against tobacco and silk, ornament and dress—he cuts off an important branch of useful commerce, while he loses no opportunity of snubbing and discouraging the unorthodox trader." The foreign traveler had railed against the bigotry of the Najdi overlords; in the decades to come, oil wealth would give this hostility to the cultivators and the stitchers greater power still.

The Saudi realm is handicapped by an official narrative of its own perfection. The rulers are invested in this version of things, one or two of the senior princes more so than the others. There are no Saudi terrorists, they are all outsiders. The radical doctrines of political Islam were not products of Wahhabism but imports brought into the country by Egyptian and Syrian adherents of the Muslim Brotherhood who had been given asylum and a new chance at a better life, but who had repaid the kingdom by indoctrinating its impressionable young men with their brand of radicalism. (The Egyptians return the favor: all was well, and secular and tolerant, in Egypt, but the Egyptians who went to Arabia in search of a livelihood came back altered by their contact with Wahhabism.) In the same vein, there are no Saudis infected with the AIDS virus, no prostitution rings, no sexual abuse of children.

This narrative is, in part, rooted in a cultural reluctance to name, and thus acknowledge, troubles. People here glide around harsh, unpleasant truths, leaving them unnamed. Then, too, there is the matter of Islam. If the Saudi realm is the gift of Islam—its land the home of the faith, its monarch the Custodian of Mecca and Medina, its unwritten constitution the Quran and the *sunna*, the tradition, of the Prophet—the blemishes of normal life are at best ignored lest they become blemishes on Islam itself. There was nothing odd or unexpected about the refusal of Saudis to accept that fifteen of the nineteen death pilots and "muscle" of 9/11 were their own. A pattern of denial and evasion runs deep. The American oil industry and the Saudi state were in truth twins; they had developed side by side, the Arabian American Oil Company the other great force alongside the Saudi monarchy. Yet a whole Saudi official history has been woven together which edits out the role of the Americans in the making, and securing, of the Saudi state. Now, all national histories are selective in what they remember and what they adorn and what they leave out, but the Saudi realm is particularly given to concealment and denial and to a comfortable, unexamined history. This makes reform doubly difficult, for a great deal of Saudi effort is expended on hiding the warts of the place.

Much has been made to me—much is made in the official discourse—about the huge numbers of students sent abroad and about the opportunity for change this holds out for the country. No doubt, years in the United States and Britain will leave their mark on untold numbers of younger Saudis; they shall be more skilled than their compatriots who had to settle for education on native soil. They shall receive the rewards of their foreign education. After a period of estrangement that followed the terror attacks of 9/11, the doors of American universities have opened once again for Saudi students. But the political impact of this education is difficult to foresee. It would be a stretch to see these students returning to transform the Saudi world. Saudis rebel, but they make their peace. In the literal and figurative senses of it, Saudis shed foreign garb and don their own when they return from foreign lands. They adjust to the limitations and peculiarities of their country; the culture takes them back and has a way of overlooking the things they might have done or said in youthful enthusiasm. Indeed, it is not uncommon to see those returning from foreign lands taking up extreme piety—a form of penance for liberties indulged in the "lands of unbelief."

I have long harbored doubts about the ability of the young to remake the system. I think of one telling case, a Saudi who broke with the country's politics in the early 1980s. He was a graduate student at an elite American institution, headstrong and bright and argumentative. He hailed from a poor Najdi hamlet, away from the palaces of princes and the polish of the Jeddah merchants. In 1981, he had done something unusually daring for a Saudi. He had published a piece in the leftist weekly *The Nation*. He wrote it under a pseudonym, Hayyan ibn Bayyan, in the form of an open letter to his country. It was a powerful piece of writing about a Saudi people "with no sense of control over their own destiny." Wealth had unsettled the country. "The sudden influx of money and foreigners is unhinging a traditional, xenophobic culture. The result is a nation on the brink of collective neurosis, while an oblivious government resolutely insists that all is well and offers doctored statistics chronicling ever-rising national wealth." The piece was written in the shadow of the Iranian upheaval of 1979, and he evoked the Iranian precedent. "Only immediate reforms can thwart future turmoil," he wrote.

"Hayyan ibn Bayyan" was a young author eager to be known and acclaimed for his work; it did not prove particularly difficult for the authorities to know his true identity. In a brutal political culture with little material cushioning, that piece of dissent would have doomed its author. But the system was forgiving. In the space of a few years, the young dissident had returned to Arabia after finishing law school in the United States. He had done so on a government scholarship. Ample room was made for him, and he was to prosper in the legal profession. No one of consequence held his moment of indiscretion against him. The costs of breaking with the system had been made clear to him, as clear as the benefits of accepting the order and its limits. This was not a man to storm the barricades against the order of power, nor was he likely to be there at the ramparts in defense of the order. The rulers did not ask for his enthusiasm. It was enough that he accepted the Saudi political world for what it was.

The Saudi world changes and it doesn't change. In early May of 2009, a Saudi blog posted a notice of Riyadh's "first TweetUp meant to gather people who use Twitter to socialize and meet face to face." The meeting was to be held in a coffee shop in northern Riyadh; the coffee shop was left unnamed. "Due to local laws we will have a female gathering in the family section and the male gathering in the singles section of the coffee shop." The new ways were breaking in, as they had been incessantly, as is inevitable in this world. But those pushing at the old order were still paying tribute to its red lines.

The "tweeters" were not bidding for sovereign power, only for the chance to partake of new and enticing things. Those men and women set to meet in that coffee shop were no threat to the primacy of Ibn Saud's surviving sons. The political life had not produced an alternative to the order of the royals. There were times when critics within the realm—and Arab spectators in Cairo, Beirut, and Damascus—thought that the laws of gravity would prevail and the realm would crack. By the first decade of the twenty-first century, the order had survived the Nasserist challenge of the 1950s and 1960s, the Khomeini decade in the 1980s, and Saddam Hussein's bid for mastery over the Persian Gulf. A good century after Ibn Saud had conquered Riyadh for his family, sons of his were still at the helm. The matrimonial bed had served Ibn Saud's reason of state. His sons, now old men, could still rule for yet another decade, and there were countless grandsons in the wings. As though to underline the frustratingly slow ways of the Saudi order, in April of 2009, Prince Talal ibn Abdulaziz, a son of Ibn Saud who had broken with his brothers in the 1960s, a "Free Prince" who had once opted for a brief exile in Cairo, was back at it again. His themes had not altered with the years. "The region is roiling with turmoil and radicalism, and I am afraid we are not prepared for that. We cannot use the same tools we have been using to rule the country a century ago." He called for a dialogue within the royal family, he wanted to prepare the country for eventual elections. "Hypocrites claim our society is unprepared for change and blame religious institutions. Certain people are pleased to hear that. We have to stop using the religious institutions as an excuse. King Abdullah is the ruler. If he wills it, then it will be done." Prince Talal, now eighty years of age, was one of eighteen surviving sons of Ibn Saud. By now the realm had grown used to his pronouncements. It was hard to know where his jealousy of his brothers in the circle of power ended and his genuine desire for reform began.

The sordid political condition of the Arab and Muslim world worked to the advantage of the House of Saud. The Saudis could gaze at the republics around them. As they thought of Libya under an odd, deranged ruler, as they pondered the dynastic succession in Syria, and the terrible bloodletting in Iran under its theocrats, they could only be glad that they had been spared the ruin of such upheavals. Saudis—particularly the ones in the Hijaz, by the Red Sea with its proximity to Egypt—once envied Egypt its modern ways and its vibrant culture in cinema and literature. The Saudis could now see the sad decline in Egyptian political and economic life. Egyptians in droves were coming to Arabia in search of livelihood, and the autocracy on the Nile had thwarted the political culture. To be sure, Saudis hadn't been given liberty, but the stability had come to acquit the realm.

Saudis had sent abroad their share of jihadists and their religious diehards, and, heaven knows, more than their share of money to all sorts of radical causes. They had been able to channel to foreign lands the wrath of the young and the disgruntled. This had been the case in the 1980s and 1990s, and there had been that self-righteous assertion in the aftermath of 9/11 that Saudi Arabia—its charities and its jihadists, its preachers and its media—had had nothing to do with this culture and this time of religious terror. But it was a matter of time that those furies would rebound on Saudi Arabia itself. The peace of the realm was shattered in mid-2003, with attacks on residential compounds that housed foreign workers. The year that followed was a worse year still. The targets included the country's oil infrastructure, and there would be no reprieve in 2005 either. Al Qaeda was now gunning for the Saudi regime itself. But the regime had ridden out the challenge. In truth, the monarchy and its survival were never at stake. The Saudi authorities would claim (and the reliable Government Accountability Office would sustain them) that the last successful terrorist attack in Saudi Arabia occurred in February 2007. The forces of order had hunted down Al Qaeda operatives, "arrested or killed, thousands of them," in the words of a 2009 GAO report. In 2008 alone, about a thousand individuals were indicted on various terrorism-related charges.

Obedience, a reluctance to venture beyond accepted norms and ways, seems so integral, so true, to the life of this realm. In October 2009, Reporters Without Borders triggered a burst of commentary within the country's intellectual and journalistic establishment. It had given Saudi Arabia a dismal rating on the matter of press freedom—a ranking of 163rd out of 175 nations, pretty close to the very bottom of the scale. (Kuwait ranked 60th, the United Arab Emirates 86th, Jordan 112th, Morocco 127th, Egypt 143rd. Only Syria in the Arab world presented a bleaker spectacle than Saudi Arabia, a rank of 165th.) I was in the country then, and it was interesting to observe the split between what the journalistic-intellectual establishment said in private and the commentary that was offered in the press. In public, there was a closing of the ranks: the country deserved better; those sitting in judgment of it did not know its ways and mores; the bleak assessment was a function of the fact that visas for foreign reporters were hard to come by. In private, a different judgment could be heard:

the country deserved the rebuke it had received; it hadn't made allowances for free inquiry; the press, big and cumbersome, stayed away from the issues that mattered.

There was no need for censorship, the wiser of my interlocutors said. The work is done by self-censorship, the limits of the accepted and the tolerable are known by one and all. The press can report on social matters—the needs of the handicapped, the ordeal of widows and divorced women, the plight of children. The political realm, by tacit agreement, is left alone. There is nothing but trouble awaiting those who venture into high matters of state.

An outsider encountering Arabia does not need the index offered by Reporters Without Borders. For me, again and again, the vastness of the land and its bleakness are steady reminders of the prohibitive costs of rebellion. In the fall of 2009, on my second visit to the country in four months, I made the journey from Jeddah to the resort town of Taif in the mountains beyond Mecca, a couple of hours away. I was traveling with a good friend and a man of Taif who knew the town. We drove past the holy city of Mecca on a highway through a desert landscape. The mountains, some five thousand feet above the plains, seemed menacingly close. The rocky hills were barren. It must have taken a herculean task to cut through the rocks. The landscape offered a reminder of the hardness of life in the Peninsula before the advent of the oil age. Man battled the elements here, and the unforgiving hills offered a silent rebuke to those who would dare go it alone. It was Mohamed bin Laden (Osama's father) who had been the contractor for this road. The work on it had begun in 1959, and it would take six long years to complete it.

The air grew softer as we made our way up through the mountains. The vegetation, not particularly lush, seemed natural to the land. The trees that would be easy to overlook in so many other lands seemed like a precious gift here, after the ride through the unrelenting plains. I had been told that Taif and its surroundings resembled the towns of Mount Lebanon in my ancestral land. But the traveling companion who made this observation for me fell into despondency and disappointment as we arrived in Taif. He hadn't been here in years; as a young boy he had gone camping with his friends in Taif. But this was now a ruined playground. Urban sprawl had claimed the green spaces of his imagination. Taif bore no resemblance to the cascading, soft hills of Mount Lebanon. A Ramada Inn was perched atop the hills, and the landscape below gave scant comfort. Thoughts of Osama bin Laden and his bands of warriors storming these hills and making their way to Mecca and beyond seemed like wild fantasies. This immense land under an eternal sky overwhelms both a rebel's call to sedition and the judgment of outsiders who—rightly—find it lacking on the scale of liberty and free expression.

The strength of the dominant order went beyond simple political loyalty. A standoff that played out in public in late 2009 between Al Qaeda in the Arabian Peninsula's second man in command, Said al-Shahri, and his own father, Ali, told volumes about the advantages of the rulers. Said had served time in Guantánamo. He had returned home and gone through the government's much-trumpeted program of rehabilitating former jihadists. But the jihad beckoned, and Said slipped across the border to Yemen. (The recidivism rate is in the range of

20 percent; the majority of jihadists return to normal life, but a determined minority dreads order and routine and is true to its calling.) Said's zeal was bottomless: he declared his own father, a retired civil servant, a *kafir*, an apostate, and an unbeliever. At an open forum in Riyadh on October 20 the father disowned his own son: "My country is more important than my son, all the more so if my son is a devil in the form of a man." Said, his father observed, "bit the hand that fed him" by breaking with the good government that secured his release from Guantánamo. The father had seven sons, he said, and six daughters, and all of them "led quiet lives and followed the straight path." This one son had gone astray, and the father prayed for his undoing.

The theological and political arguments for obedience are strong, but much stronger are those sacred cultural ones of custom and practice. The son had breached the code of the land when he broke with his own father, for this is a culture that maintains that Allah's blessing comes from the approval and the blessings of the parents. Now these diehards who answer the call of the jihad are perhaps sons without fathers in the figurative sense of things. Said was on his own, but it is hard to see him prevailing against the weight of tradition. To get at his sovereign, he had to get past his own father. The fight against the ruler was hard enough, the one against the father harder still.

Right alongside the report of this father's denunciation of his son, in the same paper on that day (*Okaz*, October 21, 2009), there was a report of a former jihadist from the town of Taif who had seen the light. He was in the rehabilitation program and had been given permission to attend the funeral of his sister-in-law, and to spend four days with his family. He was grateful, he said, to the custodians of power who returned him to the bosom of his family from the ordeal of Guantánamo. His father, too, was full of gratitude; he prayed to the Almighty to deliver the "beloved country from the schemes of the envious and the ill-wishers." This realm, which has had a way of directing its furies to distant lands, has shown resilience when these furies played out at home.

All was not quiet, to be sure. At the southern tip of the Arabian Peninsula, Yemen was reeling, claimed by deadly confrontations between an inept government and forces of secession and radicalism. The Yemeni and Saudi jihadists had found common cause. In late August 2009 one of the more influential of the younger princes, Muhammad bin Naif (a son of the minister of the interior), a man charged with running the counterterrorism effort, was slightly injured when a suicide bomber blew himself up after he had joined a group of well-wishers who had come to greet the deputy minister, as is customary during the month of Ramadan. The attack had taken place in Jeddah; the terrorist, a young Saudi, it was announced, came from the ranks of Al Qaeda in the Arabian Peninsula and was on a list of eighty-five militants wanted by the state. He had slipped into Saudi Arabia from Yemen. The bomb had been implanted in his rectum. On the prince's order, the man had not been searched, for he had claimed that he had come to turn himself in personally to Prince Muhammad. The (big) war against Al Qaeda may have been settled, but there were still bitter accounts between the forces of order and their challengers. A militant was still ready to die for his cause.

CHAPTER TWO

Blowback:
The Road to Dissension

In retrospect, the Saudi ruling bargain was radically changed by the first Gulf War of 1990–91. A country with no mass conscription had emerged unscathed from a potentially ruinous conflict. A vast American-led military coalition had rescued Saudi Arabia from Saddam Hussein's bid for mastery over the Persian Gulf, but the rescue and its terms, and the American military role that gave Arabia its lifeline, were to trigger a political crisis and a consuming national debate of deadly seriousness. By the objective measure of things, the custodians of the realm had been vindicated. It was in this vein that the Saudi monarch spoke of the Gulf War and of his decision to invite Western forces: "The Lord of glory and grandeur helped us with soldiers from all parts of the world. Many said that the presence of foreign forces was wrong. But I say it was a case of extreme necessity." There was no way, though, of staying the wrath of a neo-Wahhabi fringe inspired by that Arabian dread of the pollution of the foreign, infidel world. That dread had always lain dormant in the land, and it was to rear its head in the soul-searching and disputations triggered by this crisis.

Decreed by the rulers, given religious cover by the highest clerical authorities of the land, the American military presence was, for many Saudis, the intrusion into their midst of a power they viewed with a good measure of suspicion and cultural hostility. There were many in the intellectual and professional class who were sure that the Americans had come to stay, that the Iraqi conquest of Kuwait had given the distant power the excuse it needed to impose its dominion in the Arabian Peninsula. There were educated men and women, touched by doctrines and ideas of Arab nationalism, who believed that the entire affair—the Iraqi conquest of Kuwait and the American response to it—bore the mark of a conspiracy rigged by the Americans.

Shortly before the onset of the military campaign against Iraq, forty-three of the kingdom's best and brightest—journalists, academics, technocrats, a former minister of information—had written to their monarch in that vein. "The Saudi people," they said:

> want the foreign armadas to depart from the Gulf as soon as the conflict is settled. . . . We hope, Your Majesty, that we can confide in you our fears and the fears of our people that these navies remind us of those navies that colonized the Arabian Gulf under the pretext of protecting it, navies that enjoyed their powers here for tens of years. We fear that these forces might end up with permanent bases in our region and that we may become pawns in their hands. . . . The Saudi citizens believed that the strength of the Kingdom in men and modern equipment was on par with the best of this region, for we had devoted hundreds of billions of dollars to our armed forces. They were surprised before the rest of the world that we were incapable of checking the tyrannical Iraqi regime on

our own. Your Majesty . . . we ask for mass military conscription for all Saudis, men and women. We feel great sorrow and bitterness that we stood in such weakness before the Iraqi regime, a regime with a smaller national income than ours, and a population base that is not much larger than ours.

The fault line between the secularists of this land and those who wanted no "infidel" presence in their midst was exposed. On November 6, 1990, barely three months after Saddam Hussein had overrun Kuwait, some forty educated and professional women launched their own challenge to the kingdom's practices. They picked an issue at once symbolic of the country's restrictive ways and one sure to trigger the wrath of the diehards—the ban on women driving. The women came together in front of a Riyadh supermarket, dismissed their drivers, and drove in a convoy of cars before the police detained them. The liberal elements in the country hailed the women's courage, but the reactionaries had the upper hand: they saw in the deed a great challenge to the country's moral code, hounded the women and their husbands, and demanded their dismissal from professional positions they held.

Undeniably, the American presence had emboldened these brave women. The country was overflowing with foreign reporters; there were five hundred thousand foreign (mostly American) soldiers deployed in the Peninsula. And though on the fringe of a huge land mass, these foreign visitors had given the country a jolt. There were women soldiers in the American deployment defending this country. The Saudi women mounting a challenge to that most peculiar of prohibitions had the confidence that their deed would play out under the gaze of foreigners whose judgment mattered to the custodians of political power. The rulers stepped into the fight and imposed a temporary truce between the two warring sides. They withdrew the passports of the women who had staged the protests; they signaled their displeasure with the new assertiveness and hoped that the storm would blow over.

Reluctant as it had been to challenge the customs of its people, the state still could not do right by the religious radicals. Young men from Saudi Arabia who had gone to Afghanistan to fight for the faith had returned home eager to redeem and purify their land. There are no reliable estimates as to the number of Saudis who had participated in the jihad in Afghanistan. The low estimates are in the range of five thousand to ten thousand; other reports speak of thirty thousand. They had done God's work, they believed, but they had returned to the routine of their homeland and to public indifference. Rulers and *ulama* alike were branded as *kuffar* (apostates) by these extremists. The foreigner had "defiled" the sacred earth of Arabia, and the foreigner had to go. There was unforgiving zeal in the diehards' vision: the Shi'a minority in the Eastern Province would be decimated and the groups of Saudi "liberals" and secularists formed on the campuses of Texas and California would be swept aside in a campaign of zeal and frenzy. Traffic with the infidels would be brought to an end and those dreaded satellite dishes bringing the cultural pollution of the West would be taken down. For this to come to pass, though, the roots of the American presence had to be extirpated and the Americans themselves driven out of the country.

The modern Saudi state was no stranger to religious upheaval. But the new religious unrest had deep roots in the society; its leaders were an educated and resourceful lot. These were not drifters and cultists who rose to challenge the monarchy and the official religious class; they were scientists and professors and religious scholars and lay preachers. They were the kind of men who had risen elsewhere in the Muslim world to organize the forces of political Islam in the 1980s. They were sly in the way they phrased their concerns; they knew the West and its sensibilities. They had a feel for the audience they addressed; they spoke of democracy and civil liberties before Western audiences and offered more incendiary material for their followers at home.

No surprise, the challenge was to be mounted not by the timid Shi'a of the Eastern Province, but by zealots from within Najd itself, the heartland of the Saudi realm. Other provinces of the country, to be sure, partook of this unrest, but the "hardness" of this new era was Najdi to the core. Najd was coming into its own. Religious piety would empower the new Najdi drive. And this agitation rested on a sense of material deprivation. A decade of deficits lay behind the country; an expensive war had been fought; in current dollars the per-capita income had declined from $28,000 a year in the early 1980s to $8,000 a generation later; a state that had a $90 billion budget to allocate in 1981 had at its disposal less than $40 billion in 1994, and a paltry $30 billion in oil revenues in 1998. A rude awakening lay in store for a generation of younger Saudis.

"We love Najd and we are proud to belong to it," a Najdi who had settled in the Eastern Province says to his son in

Adama, a justly celebrated novel by the Saudi academic and liberal commentator Turki al-Hamad, published in 2003. "But we wouldn't like to live there. Najd has many children, but it doesn't feed them." This was a memory of Najd and its age-old reality. Political power and religious agitation, the oil wealth claimed by Najd and its merchants and its clerics and its notables by right of political (and religious) primacy over the Hijazis and the people of the Eastern Province, had remade the Peninsula. The Eastern Province had the oil and the access to the waters of the Persian Gulf, Hijaz had Jeddah and the holy cities of Mecca and Medina, and the window onto the Red Sea; Najd had its zeal and the conquering ethos that justified its place in the sprawling kingdom. The Sauds' base was in Najd, and the heartland of their dominion had a fierce sense of entitlement that the other communities could not match.

A new political tool was to make its appearance in the land—the petition to the rulers, the "memorandum of advice" chronicling the nation's woes, challenging the dynasty's monopoly on political power. The first petition had been that "liberal" manifesto urging the modernization of the political system. But the floodgates had been thrown wide open; the religious diehards would soon take to this new form with a vengeance. Hitherto, the ethos of Arabia had no place for collective petitions. In its lore and in its narrative of itself, Arabian society exalted the ability of the individual to have his say in the presence of authority with no need for mediation. In an ideal drawn from simpler times, a man with grievances would turn up in the *majlis* (the council, the court of a prince), put forth his claim, say his "word of truth" without fear or equivocation. The society had outgrown the intimacy of its past; its population had grown, and so had the distance between ruler and ruled. Arabia had become thoroughly urbanized; Riyadh, fifty years earlier a place of no consequence, had a population of two million by 1990. The country may have exalted the tribe, but it had been de-tribalized. The petition was a product of this new urban culture.

A landmark petition, the "memorandum of advice," turned up in September 1992. This time, 107 religious scholars and prayer leaders attached their names to it. They addressed it to the grand mufti of the kingdom, Shaykh Abdulaziz ibn Baz, the most senior figure of the religious establishment. Ibn Baz, then in his early eighties, was a traditionalist on social mores who had held the line against modernist changes, and a quietist on political matters, committed to upholding the authority of the rulers. This presented some difficulty for the Islamists. It was hard to issue a forthright denunciation of the man. He was addressed as a revered "father" even as the dissidents broke from the authority of the conservative jurists. No one was fooled: the battle had been joined. Where the custom and the practice of the polity had assigned a privileged (but hemmed in) space for the *ulama*, this new petition came close to asserting a right to political power. In a break with that old division of labor between prince and preacher, the scholars now claimed that they should be able to "oversee and participate" in the work of the ministries and embassies; they called for a powerful army of "half a million men, fired up by the spirit of jihad who would fight the Jews and help the Muslims." The political order was restrictive enough in cultural matters, but the dissidents wanted more and called for

censorship of all magazines and television programs that dis-
seminated "secular ideas."

These petitioners held the state up to its own ideals; they
called on it to enforce "what it had decreed for itself." In this
land which professed the faith, the signatories saw "blatant
violations" of God's law: television programs which promoted
"social deviance and sexual enticement," video stores which
sold "thousands, nay tens of thousands of films with explicit
sexual scenes which awaken and stir up sinful passions." This
was "Islam's land and its lodestar," yet its cultural life was lit-
tered with deviations from the faith.

In the traditional division of labor, the House of Saud had
held a virtual monopoly on foreign affairs. These people of the
"Islamic sciences" now looked on the foreign practices and alliances of the state with a jaundiced eye. There were practices
and policies of the state, traffic with outsiders, which ran afoul
of the strictures of Islam. There was the country's alliance with
the Syrian despot, Hafez al-Assad. The petitioners did not have
to name him, but the reference to him was unmistakable. Here
was a secular ruler, from an esoteric sect, the Alawites, with
dominion over an Islamic land he had broken and tormented.
This was an affront to these signatories: it was "improper" for
the kingdom, perhaps "impermissible" for it, to "sustain a tyrant
in his tyranny over an Islamic land, build privileged and close
relations with him in the fields of economy, politics, and security even though it was known that he was against God and His
Prophet and against the believers." He was not the only tyrant
that the kingdom indulged: there were others nearby with
whom normal traffic was carried out even though it was known

that they "war against Islam and oppress the believers." In the foreign world, this kingdom had no choice: it had to adhere to Islam and seek to "render it victorious." There may have been a measure of decorum in the petition, but the very "ruling bargain" of the realm was being contested.

Whether he wanted it or not, Ibn Baz was at the center of things: the dissidents were turning to him in the name of tradition and purity and all those militant ideas that were innate to the Wahhabi creed. But the rulers, and the peace of the land, had their call on him and it was with the order that he would side. The old mufti assembled his council of establishment jurists and issued a stern denunciation of the memorandum of advice on September 17, 1992. He was keen to distance himself from the memorandum. It was not true, the senior jurists said, that Ibn Baz had approved the petition or associated himself with it. Those who prepared the memorandum had only worked to "promote dissension, implant spite, concoct defects, or exaggerate them." The "good deeds" of the state had been overlooked and the petition had become a "devious tool for malicious enemies." It was permissible, and within the bounds, to render advice to the rulers. But such advice had its rules: it had to be "sincere" and it had to "emanate from a desire to secure unity and keep away the factions that sow dissension. When condemning this memorandum, we don't claim perfection. We pray to God to enable our rulers to do what pleases Him and to do what is proper and right for the people and the country. We also pray to God to enable all the Muslim rulers and all the people of Islam to do all that is good."

For Ibn Baz and the senior jurists, this had not been an easy verdict to issue. Of a group of seventeen of the country's highest religious authorities, seven had not signed this ruling and were recorded "absent for medical reasons." There were cracks in the consensus. The dissenters had exposed the fissures in the religious class and the tension at the heart of the dominant creed in the land between the desire for order and stability on the one hand and the passion of Wahhabism on the other.

The religious institution and its custodians had done well by the monarchy. There had been nothing here of the campaign that the Pahlavi dynasty had waged against the *ulama* in Iran—a steady attack on their prerogatives and turf, a centralizing drive that made the men of religion feel shabby and archaic in their own land. There had been no "reforms" akin to the ones which the Egyptian state had launched in the 1960s, which had shackled that country's official religious institution and stripped it of its autonomy and power. Shrewd and worldly, the jurists knew that *mulk* (sovereignty), the power of the sword, was essential to the survival of the religious institution that Arabia had in place. The jurists knew the primacy of the ruler, the advantages of his sword and his treasure. A tale of the realm left no doubt about the ruler's ascendancy: it was told that the very mild and genial King Khalid (ruled 1975–82) had once said that the *ulama* were on his head (a sign of respect), but were he to shake his head they would fall to the ground.

The ramparts thrown up by the dominant political-religious order were breached. In 1993, a group of dissidents launched a movement by the name of Committee for the Defense of Legitimate Rights. Its founders were six men drawn

34

from the judiciary and the professions. The oldest of the lot was a religious judge, Abdullah Masaari, a man who had been a classmate of the grand mufti himself. He was old and distinguished enough to claim a special badge of honor: he had known the legendary founder of the dynasty, Ibn Saud. He had been close, it was said, to the revered King Faisal, the third ruler of the kingdom. The spokesman for this group was Abdullah Masaari's son, Muhammad, a German-trained physicist who had lived in the United States and was married to an American. There was a Janus-like quality to this group. It wrapped itself in classic civil libertarian banners as it outflanked the monarchy on matters of Islamic governance.

The state struck back: the members of this group were arrested. After a brief imprisonment, the physicist quit the country and turned up in London. In his new home, he persisted with his oppositional politics. He was away from his native land, but he had the modern means of communication: the fax, the long-distance telephone. And he had the world of London, and the traffic of the Arabs in that city, and the Arabic journalism.

The real struggle was at home, though. The temper of the land, and the deadly nature of the political-religious contest, could be read into a booklet that Ibn Baz issued in 1993 on the relations between ruler and ruled and on the propriety and legality of foreigners residing and working in Arabia. Written in an accessible question-and-answer form, there is little subtlety in the issues addressed by Ibn Baz. The jurist takes up the matter of *khuruj* (rebellion) against the political authorities and its permissibility. He all but writes off the possibility that any good can come out of rebellion. Even the "unjust sultan" is to be tolerated; the community is best advised to "enjoin the good and forbid evil," for it has no way of knowing whether a "greater evil" awaits those who opt for rebellion.

And here is vintage Ibn Baz on the deadly serious matter of safety for the foreigners in Arabia:

> Q: Some young people think that enmity toward unbelievers and infidels who live or visit in Muslim lands is legal and decreed, and that it's permissible to kill them and loot their property if they were to do forbidden things.
>
> A: It is impermissible to kill the unbelievers who had been given a pledge of safety by the state; it is impermissible to commit aggression against them. Such people, when they err, must be referred to the rule of the *sharia* (Islamic law).

Two deeds of terror would give these theological ruminations a brand-new seriousness. The first took place in Riyadh in November 1995: a car bomb struck an American training facility for the Saudi National Guard, killing five Americans. A more devastating deed of terror took place in the oil town of Dhahran in June 1996. This time, a housing facility for American military personnel was hit; nineteen American servicemen were killed and more than four hundred were wounded as they rested in their dormitory. The American contingent in Dhahran was there to monitor the "no-fly zone" over southern Iraq, which had been put in place in the aftermath of the military campaign against Saddam Hussein. The "splendid isolation" of Arabia, perhaps made more tranquil by the telling, had been brought to a cruel reckoning.

Ibn Baz and his colleagues in the religious establishment had an urgent new task before them: the rulers and the peace of their realm needed religious warrant. Ibn Baz was to supply it in a *fatwa* he issued after the attack in Dhahran. The deed, he said, was a "transgression against the teachings of Islam." But the jurist tipped his hand: in the ruling, the words "America" and "Americans" do not appear. The damage to lives and property befell many people, "Muslims and others alike." These "non-Muslims" had been granted *aman*, a pledge of safety; they were owed protection. The shaykh found enough scripture and tradition to see a cruel end for those who pulled off the "criminal act." There was a *hadith*, a saying, a tradition, attributed to the Prophet: "He who killed an ally will never know the smell of paradise." And there was the word of God in the Quran: "Those that make war against Allah and his apostle and spread disorder in the land shall be put to death or crucified or have their hands and feet cut off on alternate sides; or be banished from the country. They shall be held to shame in this world and sternly punished in the next" (5:33–34).

Ibn Baz permitted himself a decent drapery: there was no need to acknowledge that the Americans were present in large numbers in Arabia. The welcome for the Americans was wearing thin. Even hard-core expats who once loved the order and the perks and the life in the compounds were unnerved by a new hostility. The Americans were encountering a new belligerence in the shopping malls; there were young religious militants now turning up at the gates of the compounds to stare down and bully the Americans. The fire, and the prohibitions, of Wahhabism were astir. They were there in Ibn Baz, but held in check.

A fault line, at once generational and cultural, had emerged in Arabia. Possessed of new wealth and eager for the skills of the modern world, tens of thousands of Saudis had been sent abroad for higher education in the universities of the West in the 1960s and 1970s. They had returned home to man the new bureaucracy and to prosper in the private sector. They had done well by the West and felt no great disjunction in their world. But a population boom hit Arabia in the mid-1970s (the country's birthrate, 3.8 percent a year, was one of the highest in the world), and this generation was to stay at home. The country had built its own universities; there was less wealth around for scholarships abroad. The curricula of these universities gave pride of place to religious subjects. The skills and the advantages of the generation of the oil boom could not be passed on to those large numbers of young people coming into their own in the 1980s and 1990s.

Wealth had altered the age-old balance between man and the land. Those desert and farming towns in Qasim—a fertile belt of Central Najd, which now seemed to have more than its share of religious dissidents—had become cities in their own right. Qasim's most consequential urban center, Buraida, some two hundred miles north of Riyadh, was by the early 1990s a city of nearly three hundred thousand. In the chroniclers' accounts of a century earlier, when the "penetration of Arabia" began, Buraida had been a town of some seven thousand inhabitants. The facts of Buraida, before the age of oil, were simple and timeless. There was water "at the depth of a camel stick." By the measure of the harsh desert world at its edge, Buraida was prosperous and settled, living off its wheat fields and palm groves. There was also its location on the trade and pilgrimage routes to Mecca and Medina. Buraida's people had been shrewd about religious and worldly matters: alternately fierce and accommodating, moving back and forth between the call of the faith and their worldly needs. Acquisitive and curious, the people of Buraida had been good at pressing both their worldly and their religious claims. The agitation that erupted in Buraida in September 1994—demonstrations were held and the leaders of the dissidents were imprisoned—was in keeping with Buraida's style.

There is an image of Najd and of Central Arabia: it is partly earned, and partly a projection onto it of the need for an impenetrable realm where there is something pure and uncompromising and untouched by the world. The travelers and explorers who first went to Arabia in the late 1800s gave voice to that view and passed it onto us. Palgrave, that gifted British writer and rogue of many disguises—a one-time officer in the Indian army, then a Jesuit priest in Lebanon, a traveler who went to Arabia in 1862–63 posing as a Syrian Christian physician—caught and gave currency to this view, which still lives on today. "The central provinces of Nejed," he wrote:

> the genuine Wahhabi country, is to the rest of Arabia a sort of lion's den, on which few venture and yet fewer return. *Hada Nejed; men dakhelaha f'ma Kharaj,* this is Nejed, he who enters it does not come out again, said an elderly inhabitant of whom we had demanded information; and such is really very often the case. Its mountains, once the fortresses of robbers and assassins, are at the present day equally or even more formidable as the strongholds of fanatics who consider

every one save themselves an infidel or a heretic, and who regard the slaughter of an infidel or a heretic as a duty, at least a merit.

Palgrave had come to Najd during a time of troubles. A cholera epidemic had broken out; the zealots had taken this as a sign of divine disfavor and had set out to uproot the deviations and the vanities. Tobacco had vanished from the markets; "torn silks strewed the streets or rotted on the dunghills; the mosques were crowded and the shops deserted." By the outer appearances of things, the zealots armed with "rods and Qurans" had imposed their utopia. But even as he depicted the stern Najd of the holy warriors, Palgrave lets us see the cracks: orthodoxy, he wrote, was "destined to meet with but a partial triumph. A compromise now took place, dresses wherein silk should not exceed a third part, or at most a half of the material, were permitted, though with a sigh; tobacco vendors or smokers were henceforth content with observing decent privacy in the sale or consumption of the forbidden article, on which condition they might do as they choose, unmolested, save in the public streets or marketplace. Compulsory attendance at prayers was rarely enforced . . . "

The self-sufficiency of that desert world was never whole and unalloyed to begin with: the merchant caravans, and the trade routes, and the workers from Qasim who could be found, in the late 1800s, as far away as the Suez Canal, bear witness to that. "For a consideration," the Wahhabi warriors in Palgrave's time allowed the passage through their domain of the "heretics" of Persia to the holy cities of Mecca and Medina: it took "eighty gold tomans" per Persian pilgrim to guarantee the travelers immunity from danger and pillage.

The temptations of the world have grown by leaps and bounds in that long stretch of time that separates us from Palgrave and from the Wahhabi warriors of that simpler age. The satellite dishes in Najd were not about to be taken down. There was enough cunning in that world of Central Arabia to permit a stern visage in public and plenty of backsliding in the shadows. Arabia had once been largely desolate, its history an unbroken spectacle of brigandage and disorder. The vast territories had been knit together—a subcontinent, for all practical purposes— by right of conquest. Order had come, and men had made their peace with it. The Peninsula's truth could have come straight out of the pages of Thomas Hobbes's *Leviathan*: a "commonwealth by acquisition" had emerged in the land. It had provided order where there had been insecurity of life and of possession. "And though of so unlimited a Power, men may fancy many evil consequences, yet the consequences of the want of it, which is the perpetual warre of every man against his neighbor, are much worse." There was a measure of unrest in the land, to be sure. But the realm held together because of that deeper knowledge that the zealots could not rule, that their rods and their anger would throw the place back into its dreaded past.

Ibn Baz and the traditional jurists arrayed around the dynasty knew the history of their land: the first Saudi state (1744–1818) had burned with fury and zeal and had self-destructed. The purists had risen in Najd but had tempted the fates. In the isolation of Najd, the Wahhabis had been no threat to the rule of the Ottoman authorities. But conquest and the zeal of a stern religious creed had tugged at them. They overran Hasa on the Persian Gulf, then they struck into Iraq. In 1802, Wahhabi raiders sacked the Shi'a holy city of Karbala. They killed some five thousand of its people and leveled its shrines, including the tomb of the Prophet's grandson, Shi'ism's iconic figure Imam Hussein. The attack on Karbala was a blow to the prestige of the Ottoman state. But more was to come, and on more sensitive terrain still. In 1802–4, the Wahhabis ventured into the Hijaz. They overran the holy cities of Mecca and Medina and brought to that worldly part of the Peninsula a reign of ter-ror and religious rigor. The pilgrimage was interrupted by the zealots; the claim of the Ottoman caliph to sovereignty over the holy cities was being challenged by the Wahhabis.

A Wahhabi empire beckoned. And the warriors paid no heed to the British interest in the sea lanes and the coastal lands of the Gulf. A "political resident" in the Persian Gulf oversaw "maritime peace" and the safety of the trade routes to India. The Wahhabis, bent on dominating Central Arabia and the coastal lands alike, violated the British red lines. The fall of this Wahhabi dominion was quick to come. Foreign interven-tion in 1817–18—an Egyptian expeditionary force on behalf of the Ottoman imperial state—laid their towns and fortresses to waste, killed or imprisoned their leaders. Faith had not been enough. And faith—this kind of blind fury—was sure to lead to even greater ruin today. A skilled hand was needed to keep the oil flowing, to carry on traffic with the world beyond.

The outline of the realm's history has been repeatedly told: the reconquest (the third attempt by a new generation) of the Peninsula by Abd al-Aziz Ibn Saud, a young man who had spent his youth in Kuwait, under the protection of that principality's ruling family. He had relied on the townsmen and the sedentary communities of Najd in Central Arabia; religious enforcers had been crucial to the establishment of the realm. Another instrument had been crucial in the early history of this expanding Saudi state, the Ikhwan (literally "the brothers," a religio-tribal corps), who came to serve as the shock troops of this new order. The Ikhwan had been drawn from tribesmen who had been brought into the fold of Islam and instructed about the faith by the religious specialists. The discipline of a religio-political order warred with the anarchy of their old ways. It was a state that these Ikhwan had helped build, and a state ran counter to their deepest impulses.

Their work of conquest done by the mid-1920s, the Ikhwan had begun to bristle under the new system of control. On the borders of this new Pax Saudica, there was British power—in the sea lanes and coasts of the Persian Gulf, and in neighboring Jordan and Iraq. Ibn Saud understood the magnitude of British power, and indeed sought its patronage. The Ikhwan could not accept this order of states and national boundaries; in truth, they had grown uncomfortable with the regimentation of state power. The new order provided some opportunities for agricultural work, but these tribesmen disdained it. They had conquered more worldly, more settled people (the luxury-loving Hijazis, the Shi'a agriculturalists and merchants in the Eastern Province), but now they had to let those communities be.

Ibn Saud wanted order in the new dominions. He needed loans from the merchants of Jeddah, and he needed tranquility in the holy cities of Mecca and Medina lest the image of his realm be damaged in the wider world of Islam. He would not let loose these warriors on his new provinces. The Ikhwan were literalists; having been given the faith by their mentors, they had set out to enforce it in newly conquered lands.

In vain, Ibn Saud had tried to rein in these warriors. On one occasion, he reminded them of his rights—and power—over them: "Beware, oh Ikhwan. Encroach not upon the rights of others. If you do, your value and that of the dust are the same." The sword decided the matter. In a seminal, defining battle for the new realm on March 29, 1929, at a desert patch by the name of Sibila in northern Najd, Ibn Saud's forces overwhelmed the Ikhwan. The three tribal confederations that provided the Ikhwan with their backbone—the Ajman, the Mutair, the Utaybi—were broken. The age of raiding had drawn to a close.

The state had had its way. What opposition erupted in the years to come was of the secular, nationalist variety that was the fashion of the 1950s and 1960s. But the fury that had given rise to the Ikhwan was too deep and innate to the land to simply disappear. Five decades later, Juhayman al-Utaybi, a former corporal in the National Guard, a Bedouin with rudimentary education, then in his early forties, pulled off an audacious deed: he and some three hundred of his followers seized the Grand Mosque in Mecca. It was November 20, 1979, and by the lunar calendar, the dawn of a new Islamic century.

Juhayman had parodied the Ikhwan: the sandals, the shin-length *thoub*, a flowing, unkempt beard. His themes were straight out of those warriors who had been cut down half a century earlier: the corruption of the rulers, the "pollution" of the realm due to its traffic with infidels. In an odd twist, Juhayman had called on the fifty thousand pilgrims who were trapped in the Grand Mosque to declare his brother-in-law the *mahdi* (savior) of the present age.

The notion of the *mahdi* is integral to the Shi'a worldview, while Sunni Islam is silent on it. But this was not an orderly, or an "orthodox," religious movement. It was a millenarian rebellion harking back to an early golden age, driven by rage at everything that the modern state had built. Its leader was apocalyptic and deranged. In "seven letters" which he had addressed to the faithful, Juhayman had prophesied that the main battle for Islam would be fought in Constantinople, with horses and swords. He was an avenger; he had risen to claim vindication for the Ikhwan, "may God rest their souls," who had given Al Saud their dominion, "conquered the country" for them only to be betrayed. Ibn Saud's betrayal, he said, had been accomplished with the help of the Christians; acquisitive and supplicant *ulama* had acquiesced in that betrayal, and people had become "ignorant of the ways of Islam." The scholars may possess religious knowledge, the rebel had opined, but what they knew they utilized in the service of corrupt rule. The wealth of the land, its oil, was being wasted, bartered for American protection. Juhayman would follow the Prophet's example: there would be vigilant warfare and propagation of the faith.

Juhayman's revolt was doomed. It had offended the faithful by violating the sanctity of the Grand Mosque. But Juhayman had unnerved the rulers. It took two weeks to flush the rebels out of the mosque. Religious warrant was sought for a police incursion into the Grand Mosque. French advice and help had been secured; quietly, officers and units of the Groupe d'Intervention de la Gendarmerie were dispatched to the scene. The rebel had been a genuine embarrassment to the state. He and sixty-two of his followers were dispatched to eight of the kingdom's cities, where they were beheaded.

It was not just the rebellion of Juhayman and the phantom ghost of the Ikhwan that had unsettled the dynasty. Four years earlier, a modernizing monarch, King Faisal, who had prodded his country along by giving legitimacy to women's education, television, and travel to foreign lands, had been struck down by an assassin from within the House of Saud itself. It was a fight over the introduction of television that had set the stage for the monarch's murder. And at the dawn of this new Islamic century, a turbaned, fierce revivalist, Ayatollah Ruhollah Khomeini, had ridden mass discontent to great power in nearby Iran.

There was no kingship in Islam, Khomeini asserted, and this Islam in the Peninsula was only "American Islam," an instrument of the Great Satan. The Saudi rulers had always held the Shi'a minority in the Eastern Province in great suspicion, and now in November of 1979—the very month of the upheaval in Mecca—trouble came to the Shi'a towns of that province. Quiescent men hitherto content to live their lives away from the gaze of the authorities took to the streets in the city of Qatif after a confrontation with the police during a celebration of Ashura, the annual ritual of mourning for Imam Hussein. The demonstrators were not a threat to the survival of the regime, but a threshold of fear had been crossed. No mercy would be shown them. The helicopter gunships of the National Guard would be called into action. True to their worldview and their practice, the rulers were quick to see in these protests the fine hand of their Iranian rivals. The example supplied by Iran—the spectacle of militant Shi'ism—was no doubt a factor, but these protests were a response to the material and psychic disinheritance of the Shi'a. There was widespread deprivation in the Shi'a towns, and there was the sense fostered by the Wahhabi creed itself that the Shi'a of the country were outcasts and heretics.

The sense of political mastery and control on the part of the rulers had given way. It was in the grip of this uncertainty that the monarchy chose to outflank the new puritanism, and take it onto itself. It was in the time of the "armed *imam*" in Qom that the monarch of the Saudi state would claim the title of Khadim al-Haramain al-Sharifain, Custodian of the Two Holy Mosques, to emphasize the religious dimension of his authority. (The reference is to the holy cities of Mecca and Medina.) And it was in this turbulent era that a discernible retreat from modernism took place. Juhayman had been beheaded, but he had frightened the rulers and had demonstrated the dangers of modernism. The radical preachers grew more emboldened, and the technocratic Western-oriented elite became increasingly uncertain of itself and of its own world.

In the age of scarcity and hunger—there were older Saudis who still remembered that locusts were a source of protein in a harsh, unforgiving world—there had been a yearning for progress. A chronicle from the early 1920s documented a crippling poverty unimaginable in today's Arabia. In Riyadh, hundreds of people came to the ruler's palace twice a day, in the morning and in the afternoon, for two square meals. Concealed under the *abayas* of some of them were "kettles or wooden platters for the

purpose of taking some rice and lamb to their kith and kin outside the city." A talented physicist born in the early 1960s, with
an American doctorate (three of his brothers have advanced
American degrees), told me of his father making the journey in
the late 1930s from one of the villages of Qasim to Riyadh. The
journey took this man's father nine days; he attached himself
to a caravan, or tried to do so, to be more precise. The leaders of the caravan did not want the additional burden, another
mouth to feed. They administered a harsh beating or two to this
unwanted companion of the road. But the young man persisted;
it was this caravan or the risk of death from thirst and hunger.
Today, this passage would be made in an air-conditioned car; it
would take five or six hours. Yet amid this sudden, new prosperity, there was grief and a brittle kind of anger. The new religious unrest grieved for a world that an earlier generation had
been eager to escape.

The trail of sedition had been blazed by a respectable
kind of critic: a scholar at a religious institution, Umm al-Qura
University in Mecca, by the name of Safar al-Hawali. He was
forty-one years of age when fame came his way in the tumult
that followed Saddam Hussein's invasion of Kuwait. This was
not a man to follow an official line. He belonged to a respectable tribe in the southwestern part of the country, by the
resort town of Taif. He had had a thorough preparation for his
role: he had been a child prodigy in religious studies. In the
holy cities of Mecca and Medina, he had earned a doctorate.
Along the way, he had written treatises against secularism and
secularists. In 1990–91, he stepped outside the bounds of the
religious academy. It was a speech in a Riyadh mosque, we are

told by an admiring chronicler, that had helped spread this man's fame.

In that speech, Hawali condemned Saddam Hussein's conquest of Kuwait, as was obligatory during that menacing time for the Saudi state. But the startling surprise lay in what he said about the American forces that were there with the dynasty's blessing and permission: "The Baath of Iraq is the enemy of this hour, while the Americans and the Franks are our enemy until Judgment Day." Hawali challenged the silence of the realm. Half-learned in Western sources, stitching together citations from authoritative Western periodicals, Hawali warned that "the Crusaders" had come to stay. In a book-length letter he addressed to the highest jurist in the country, Shaykh Abdulaziz ibn Baz, he saw the coming of the Americans as a fulfillment of his worst fear, as something scripted and inevitable: "I have been fearing something like this ever since the beginning of this so-called détente between East and West and the unity of Crusading Europe under one banner. This has been a bigger calamity than I had expected, bigger than any threat the Arabian Peninsula had faced since God Almighty had created it." The Americans, he wrote, had always wanted dominion over the Peninsula, and now they had achieved what their hearts had desired. This was no ordinary military intervention but one that aimed at changing the country and its mores, "particularly on the matter of women's rights."

Hawali had cut to the heart of the matter. His country's code—the seclusion of women, the restrictions on their right to travel, to drive cars, to move about in a normal way—was threatened by the American example and the American presence. For

Hawali, the landing of this alien army in the Peninsula was an event on par with the great thrusts that the West had made into Islamic lands, a successor invasion to the Crusades in the Middle Ages and to the "Age of Western Discovery" of the East in the 1500s. How else could one account, he asked, for the hubris of the invaders, for the way they belittle the land and its religion and its people and its *ulama* and its rulers? This was no rescue that America offered: "A huge army of five hundred thousand soldiers have been dispatched to the Arabian Peninsula and the Gulf, thirty thousand of them women, and an undeclared number of Jews who had Israeli rabbis performing ceremonies on the sacred earth of the Arabian Peninsula."

Rebellions always entail a good measure of contagion: a dissident steps forth from the shadows, better yet a respectable sort, then others who had been nursing quiet grievances are emboldened. In no time, there emerged some other dissidents of note: Salman al-Awda, a lecturer in the Najdi city of Buraida; Ayid al-Qarni, a lecturer from the city of Abha, in the southwest; Muhammad ibn Saad al-Qahtani from Umm al-Qura University in Mecca, etc. Some fifty men—preachers, *imams* (mosque leaders), judges, academics drawn from the nation's universities—came forth in May 1991 with a petition addressed to King Fahd. The petitioners spoke as loyal men of the state, eager to keep at bay foreign predators and foreign influence: they called for the building of a "powerful army, equipped from a variety of sources" and for a foreign policy that "guarantees the interests of the *umma* (the Islamic community) and keeps it away from alliances which contradict the *sharia*." And the petitioners spoke as men of reform: they wanted "forthright conduct and honesty from all state officials." This was a shot across the bow, and a battle was not far behind.

The most radical of this group of politicized preachers was Shaykh Salman al-Awda. He was to become Hawali's partner in the ideological war that had been sparked by the coming of the Americans. A label of honor was given Hawali and Awda by the throngs that bought their audiocassettes and leaflets, crowding the prayer halls where they spoke: they were dubbed Shuyukh al-Sahwa, the Shaykhs of the Awakening. Five years younger than Hawali, Awda had received his education at Buraida, then moved on to Riyadh, to the Imam Mohammad Ibn Saud Islamic University, where he studied the *sharia*. For his graduate degree he wrote a thesis with a title suggestive of zeal to come, "Ghurbat al Islam," referring to the exile or the absence of Islam. (This theme of Islam's estrangement and solitude even in the lands which nominally profess the faith is dear to the Islamists and would recur in Awda's audiocassette tapes and printed lectures.) Restless and eloquent, this preacher had an unerring instinct for the seam between the religious and the political: to judge by the tone and content of his tapes, he had in him the combined talents of the storyteller and the caller's zeal. Thousands would flock to his sermons, he was in demand everywhere, his opinions sought after and at the ready.

His one big theme was corruption—not the small type that afflicts princes and bureaucrats but the corruption that overtakes nations and brings about their downfall, the corruption that eats into a society and implicates its people in great deviations. In the face of such corruption, the believer has no choice, Awda exhorted. In matters large and small, the believer has to speak out "against the corruption taking root in our country and, to varying degrees, in all Muslim lands." The road to reform was not strewn with roses but with thorns. It was "not enough to eat and drink and move about"; a whole generation of educated people owed it to itself, and to the wealth spent giving it new skills, to speak out about the sad state of affairs in public life. Awda knew the risks, and he drew a marker for the rulers: he was not concerned with the threat of imprisonment, he said. The cause of Islam was transcendent and the political realm was capricious at any rate. No one, he said, knew why political prisoners are rounded up and why they are released. He trusted his fate to the Almighty; he left it to Him to dispose of this "weak creature."

Hawali and Awda tested the rulers' patience and skills. It was not easy to silence these men. There were serious jurists, men of the religious establishment, who gave these two firebrands their support and their approval. They were not extremists, an authoritative cleric of the realm, Abdullah ibn Jibrin, said of them. They were well intentioned and fought for the faith. They were a "thorn in the side of the Christians, the Communists, the atheists, the Ba'athists, the secularists, the polytheists." They knew the tricks of the "heretics" (read: the Shi'a) and the apostates, and it was no wonder their enemies had seen fit to besmirch their reputations. The most authoritative traditionalist of the religious class, the revered Abdulaziz ibn Baz, weighed in on the side of the two men: they were not infallible, he said, but they meant well. They had not strayed from the path; their "tapes were useful" and free of heresy and sedition. The dissenters had stayed within the bounds of the dominant tradition, and this gave them no small shelter.

There is a great "empiricism" to this desert world: you have to tell the difference between a mirage and the real thing if you are to survive in the desert. And this seemingly theological struggle took place against the background of dwindling riches in the country and of a fight over wealth and subsidies and material benefits. Two decades earlier, God's *baraka* (blessing) had been expressed in the windfall fortune that flooded the country after 1973. Now recession and retrenchment had come, and this new austerity was seen as proof of the withdrawal of divine grace. The patronage system was breaking down. Public debt had begun to rear its head. Three years into these troubles, the state had had its fill.

The crackdown came in September 1994. More than one hundred politico-religious dissidents—Hawali and Awda at the head of the pack—were taken into custody. The two firebrands were given a choice: they could cease their preaching and admit their errors, or face imprisonment. They chose the latter course. When the state finally struck back, it was keen to have religious cover. The writ for their arrest was wrapped inside a ruling by the Council of Higher Ulama. The old traditionalist himself, Shaykh Abdulaziz ibn Baz, was for all practical purposes turned into a partner to this deed. It couldn't have been a happy choice, but the old scholar obliged. He served the state, and the rulers had come calling in the midst of mounting disorder. He called on Hawali and Awda to apologize for their "excesses" and to cease their agitation.

The state would make the most of Ibn Baz's support. The authority of "His Eminence the Grand Mufti of the Kingdom, Shaykh Abdulaziz ibn Abdullah ibn Baz" was attached to the judgment of the Ministry of Interior. Ibn Baz knew the wages of riding with the rulers. He gave his writ knowing that younger, more radical preachers had begun to brand him, with his senior colleagues, as *ulama al-sulta*, the scholars of the regime. But he had a whole jurisprudence to fall back upon: in his doctrine sedition was a greater evil than tyranny, and rebellion knew no legitimacy.

The faith had to be capped. In the view of the religious establishment, it was the proper thing to "enjoin the good and forbid evil," but it was imperative to do so with restraint. Shaykh Saleh bin Abdulaziz al-Shaykh, who was the minister of Islamic affairs and endowment and guidance (and a direct descendant of the eighteenth-century preacher Muhammad ibn Abdul Wahhab), found a tradition attributed to the Prophet Muhammad that a judge cannot render binding rulings when he is in a state of agitation. For this conservative jurist, the call to the faith had to be made, but without stridency and belligerence.

The state that had hauled off the religious dissidents to prison now set out to display its own fidelity to the faith. It would try to outflank these dissidents on their own terrain. It was out of this struggle and its dangers that a parallel strategy was born whose consequences would be there for everyone to see a decade hence. The zeal was channeled to foreign lands: there were pan-Islamic duties that exonerated that state and gave its brand of religion a new legitimacy. There were religious obligations in Palestine and Bosnia and Chechnya and Afghanistan. Religious merit would be gained in those zones of battle. A mosque to be built in Rome, a mission of rescue in Bosnia against the enemies of Islam: the faith served and fortified beyond Arabia's borders. The philanthropies, and the preachers, and the restless young in search of an outlet for their zeal would be encouraged to look to those places as new battlegrounds.

The ennui of the youth, bottled up at home, would find satisfaction in other lands. And the "good works" in those lands would offer proof that here was a political order that looked after Islam where its truth, or its peoples, were under assault. The work of *da'wa* (the call to religion) knew no borders; a state that spread it abroad could not and should not be subverted at home. This land had known rebellions and had seen them blow over. It had an unsentimental faith in property and old age and responsibility, and the prince's favor. It was hoped that this new zeal, too, would give way and come to terms with the established order of things.

It had worked this way with one challenger to the dynasty: the physicist Muhammad Masaari, who had been hounding the monarchy from London. Three years into exile, his effort had fizzled out; he was in debt and living on social security. "It is no secret; I am broke and I am not going to lie about it," he said in January 1997. Masaari owed money to his lawyer, who had successfully appealed a deportation decision by the Home Office, some to British Telecom, some to Feature Fax for the messages he had been sending back home. What the Egyptian-American scholar Mamoun Fandy aptly described as "cyberresistance" had been a nuisance and nothing more.

The Arabic press carried news of Masaari's bankruptcy. The message was not subtle: the wealth of the realm and of the ruler, the impossible odds against the dissident. The rulers knew their land and its ways; they left it to their people to judge these odds and to weigh the protagonists.

In the time of oil, *fi zaman al-naft*, the ruler not only provided protection and order but, of course, allocated the treasure of the land. When a relative windfall, higher oil prices in 1996, materialized and brought to Saudi Arabia some $10 billion in unexpected revenues, the rulers proceeded to pay off some of the private debts and the arrears that had accumulated over the preceding years. Some $1.8 billion was handed out to the farmers (the Qasimis must have received a fair share of the spoils). More subsidies would be paid in the year to come, they were assured.

Masaari's challenge was easy to turn back. While the physicist was in London granting interviews to Western journalists, a wholly different challenge was gathering force. Its leaders were made of sterner stuff, its recruits ready to die and kill in pursuit of their own cruel utopia. It was past the fax machines and the petitions. A year after Masaari conceded his defeat, a man of the city of Jeddah, Osama bin Laden, and a physician who belonged to the upper reaches of Egyptian society, Ayman Zawahiri, announced the launching of a new movement, the World Islamic Front for Jihad against the Jews and the Crusaders. It came in a call to arms published in a London-based Arabic daily, *Al-Quds Al-Arabi*, in February 1998. These two men were without qualms about terror and its efficacy. They sought no interviews with Western reporters; not for them was the language of human rights and the method of petitioning the rulers. A violence of unprecedented ferocity lay in store for people in Arabia and lands beyond.

The late 1990s were the era of globalization. No one would pay Bin Laden's declaration of war much attention. In the zeitgeist of the era, the time of ideology had passed and the gurus of the market and of globalization were ascendant. A band of Arabs in the forlorn land of Afghanistan was of no interest at the time. It fell to the distinguished historian of Islam Bernard Lewis to see the declaration for what it was: a license to kill and a declaration of a new jihad. Bin Laden's starting point was the American presence in his homeland. In prose of great beauty and power, the self-styled jihadist evoked the defiling presence of the United States in Arabia, the holiest of Islam's territories. "Since God laid down the Arabian Peninsula, created its desert, and surrounded it with seas, no calamity has ever befallen it like these crusaders that have spread in it like locusts, crowding its soil, eating its fruits, and destroying its verdure; and this is at a time when the nations contend against the Muslims like diners jostling around a bowl of food." Bin Laden was not a cleric, but this was the new way of the faith, and the declaration contained this all-important *fatwa*:

> To kill Americans and their allies, both civil and military, is an individual duty of every Muslim who is able, in any country where this is possible, until the Aqsa Mosque [in Jerusalem] and the Haram Mosque [in Mecca] are freed from their grip and until their armies, shattered and broken-winged, depart from all the lands of Islam, incapable of threatening any Muslim. . . . By God's leave, we call on every Muslim who believes in God and hopes for reward to obey God's command to kill the Americans and plunder their possessions wherever he finds them and whenever he can. Likewise we

call on the Muslim *ulama* and leaders and youth and soldiers to launch attacks against the armies of the American devils and against those who are allies with them from among the helpers of Satan.

The jihadists who had made their way to Afghanistan and had found new leaders in Osama bin Laden and Ayman Zawahiri were men on the run from the security services, a disaffected breed in search of a new calling. They saw in the struggle for Afghanistan proof that holy warfare, the zeal of a "believing minority," would carry the day against larger powers given to doubt and compromises. The true believers had skipped over the role played by American weapons and Saudi governmental money and Pakistani intelligence in the defeat of the Soviet Union in Afghanistan. A sense of power came to the jihadists; Afghanistan—mountainous, possessed of an austere, harsh landscape—had fed the jihadists' conviction that their mission recalled the ordeal of early Islam and its triumph.

It had been a heady undertaking, the jihad in Afghanistan. There had been warfare and comradeship, and exposure to volunteers and preachers drawn from countless Arab and Muslim lands. Now the state was done with all that; the jihad was to be decreed and legitimized by the ruler and his religious apparatus. Consider this discourse by the minister of religious endowments, Shaykh Saleh bin Abdulaziz al-Shaykh, and the play of things is laid bare. The discourse of this establishment jurist was delivered in late 2001—after the terrors of 9/11, at a time when Saudi Arabia was under a glaring spotlight. The jihad, said this jurist, was the prerogative of the ruler; no one could second-guess *wali al-amr* (the ruler, the decision maker) as to the timing or legitimacy of declaring the jihad. Mosques, he said, were places of worship and prayer where scholars who know the faith "enjoin the good and forbid evil and rule on religious matters and perform the rituals of the faith." It was becoming harder for the state to juggle its puritanism and its alliance with the United States, the cornerstone of its policies abroad. The state had been crafty and skilled, but a profound change had taken place: large numbers of rebellious, disaffected types were now contesting the power of the state and its dominant worldview.

The old traditionalist, Grand Mufti Ibn Baz, died in 1999. And his loss would be felt as the crisis of the realm intensified. To be sure, he hadn't always had his way. But the authority and standing he had with some of the dissidents went with him into his grave. Modernism and its bearers were in retreat. The state must have reasoned that the modernists in the business class and the professions had nowhere else to go, and that the rulers could tilt toward the Islamists without incurring an appreciable political cost. In this new environment, the diehards moved about with greater confidence. A young American-educated merchant described for me the authority and swagger with which the zealots had begun to carry themselves in public life. They commanded more attention when they turned up in the *majlis* of a noted prince or provincial governor. "All you had to do was turn up with an unkempt beard and a shin-length *thoub* and your presence and demands were given greater weight," he said. He noted that the *mutawwa*, the religious enforcers, had better cars and facilities in Riyadh than did the police. He told me of a young religious enforcer who came up to him at a local hotel during a business meeting he was having with a group of Italian visitors to berate him for meeting with "infidels" and breaking bread with them. He had warded off this enforcer by telling him that these foreign visitors were there with "King Fahd's permission," that the man should take his objection to the ruler of the realm. The diehards were reshaping public life to their own preference. The relative daring with which the state had pushed through earlier modernizing endeavors was put aside. There had been fights in the history of the realm over the introduction of radio, the telegraph, and television; women's education; and the permissibility of traveling into *bilad al-kufr* (the lands of unbelief) and mixing with peoples of other faiths. The state had won those fights, but now the state was on the defensive.

"He who eats the sultan's bread fights with the sultan's sword," goes a desert maxim. There was less money to go around; the state was accumulating a huge public debt that outstripped its gross domestic product. There were farmers who could no longer count on subsidies; there were contractors who had not been paid money owed them by the state treasury. More important, there were young people whose claims and expectations could no longer be satisfied. Something new and alien to the land had begun to occur in this country: there were reports of four hundred suicides, principally among the young, in the year 2000. The old world and its verities were being undermined. In hushed tones, and in the privacy of their homes and gatherings, the modernists spoke of the necessity of taking on the religious diehards. Some even harked back to the battle of Sibila in 1929, when Ibn Saud had cut the Ikhwan to shreds and turned back their challenge to the authority of the state. But the political order and the dynasty opted for accommodating the religious current.

This dynasty abhorred and dreaded hard decisions. Besides, "reform" had its own hazards. The small group of princes—and a handful of old trusted advisers around them—who ruled the kingdom had for years been fixated on the fate of the Shah of Iran, Muhammad Reza Pahlavi. In the years of his splendor and power, the occupant of the Peacock Throne had treated the Saudi dynasty as a relic of an old, doomed political world. He was a modernizer and a secularist, and he had in mind turning his country into an "Asian Germany," herding his population, kicking and screaming, into modernity. An influential member of the dynasty was given to a memory he savored, and he recited it endlessly as a reminder of what befalls those who run ahead of their people, or administer to them profound cultural shocks. In the early 1970s, the shah had written a note to his Saudi counterpart, King Faisal. The note had in it the pride of a man sure of his primacy. The Saudi monarch was advised that he had better opt for modernizing his traditional, hidebound country, reining in its religious classes, pushing it into the modern world, lest the Saudi dynasty be swept aside.

Fate was cruel to the Shah of Iran. The mullahs he offended had risen in an upheaval of enormous fury. The middle classes he had relied upon had succumbed to a wave of religious devotion of their own and had turned on him with a vengeance. The shah himself had ended up a Flying Dutchman looking for a port of call—spurned by his American allies, in search of a place that would afford him shelter for what little remained of his life. This was not a fate the House of Saud wanted for itself.

Deep down, the Saudi rulers distrusted the middle class and the Western-educated professionals, suspecting that they would desert the dynasty or duck for cover if a fight for the realm ensued. The principal men of the dynasty were without illusions about that segment of their population. There were educated, prosperous people in the country whispering sweet things about Osama bin Laden, and the rulers understood the fickle nature of men, the ease with which regimes come apart.

No descendant of Ibn Saud would embark on some hazardous new course. In the early 1960s three or four princes had such ideas. They were dubbed the "Free Princes," and they took a ride with radical Arab nationalism, hectoring their brothers from Gamal Abdul Nasser's Cairo about a new order in Arabia. But the Free Princes had come to their senses; they had been taken back into the fold. They had given up on the dream of reform; they had seen Nasser go down to defeat in 1967 and die three years later a broken man. The leading Free Prince, Talal ibn Abdulaziz, had put aside his youthful rebellion and resumed his place as a senior figure in the realm. Few Saudis believed that so difficult, so idiosyncratic a place could be reinvented.

The leading men of the dynasty were old, governed by a code of primacy and discretion and ritual transmitted to them by their legendary father, the desert chieftain Abd al-Aziz Ibn Saud. But the realm had changed. The quaint desert world had become more difficult to govern. A man of the Saudi elite, Ghazi Algosaibi, put it well in August 2002 when he said that the crisis in Saudi-American relations was an "accident waiting to happen." That accident had been heard with a big thud of course on September 11, 2001. A relationship of cold calculation of interests—American protection in return for Saudi oil—was now beset with mutual recriminations.

The congenitally secretive Saudi realm had to own up to what its world had spawned: jihadists waging war against the infidel powers, networks of financiers and "charities" which empowered the boys of terror, and a public more willing to wink at the terror and to justify it to anyone from the outside who came to inquire into the workings of the Saudi state. A measure of Saudi introspection would have been helpful, an acknowledgment of the hidden furies and dysfunctions of the realm: the boredom of the young, the quiet rage of a business class that submitted to the monarchic system and did well by it but resented its own political weakness, the intolerance of a new breed of preachers pushing at the limits of the old system of political-religious control. But this was not the Saudi way. It was easier to hunker down, alternating between righteous anger at the foreign press and the foreign scrutiny on the one hand and self-pity on the other.

One of the principal figures of the monarchy came to embody this Saudi inability and unwillingness to arrive at a reckoning with the new terror, and with the need to come clean on it all: the minister of the interior, Prince Naif ibn Abdulaziz. A full brother of King Fahd, a dour man who had held that portfolio since 1975, Prince Naif partook of the old ethos of his clan. For him, the realm was at peace, and radicalism alien to its makeup. There were no Saudis aboard those planes of 9/11, there were no "sleeper cells" of terror in Arabia. The "lobbies" in America (code word for American Jews) were out to smear the kingdom's reputation, to affix the label of terror onto Islam itself. Some "misguided" Saudi youth may have been tricked into networks of terror, but the leaders, he insisted on one occasion, came from Egypt, and the "original sin" of radicalism had been the work of elements of that country's Muslim Brotherhood. Saudi Arabia had sheltered and protected the leaders of the Brotherhood in the 1950s and 1960s when secular radicalism was the malady of the Arab world. But a trusting Arabia had been betrayed; this was the furthest this man of the royal household could go. More than an old prince's obtuseness was on display here: it was the self-image of the Saudi realm as a kingdom at peace, and a place where princes and commoners come together as a "family" immune to the call of sedition and political trouble. A choice had to be made: the realm could look inward, or it could conjure up the specter of foreign conspiracies, of enemies bent on shattering Arabia's peace. A conviction took hold in Arabia that a vast American conspiracy was being hatched against the country. Even the royals began to give credence to this view; it was an opportunity for the rulers to bond with the disaffected in their midst. A heavy dosage of anti-Americanism was seen as a sly way of buying off those disaffected with the order of power.

Saudi Arabia had not been hermetically sealed, but the kind of scrutiny that came its way after 9/11 was a plunge into a whole new world. There were foreign reporters now scouring remote hamlets in the country looking for the trail of the "death pilots." The reporters went up and down Highway 15, in the Saudi southwest, into pockets of economic neglect—twelve of the fifteen Saudis who took part in the attacks of 9/11 hailed from that part of the country. This was "Bin Laden country," the new inquiries confirmed, provinces that stretched from Mecca into the summer resort town of Taif, then climbed upward to the mountainous country of Asir. This mountainous land merited its name: Asir meant "difficult country." The windfall wealth of Arabia and the largesse of the dynasty had been sprinkled lightly around here: there was a sense of separateness that set this place apart from the Najdi heartland of the country and from the polished and skilled Hijazis. There was boredom aplenty, a forlorn hinterland, deeply tribal, and a fertile ground for the kind of religious-political radicalism Bin Laden and those preaching his message had set ablaze.

Nor were the reporters disappointed when they ventured into the worldly city of Jeddah on the Red Sea. There were tycoons and American-educated professionals (the Jeddah yuppies, a man of the Saudi state dismissively labeled them) who whispered to the reporters sweet things about Osama bin Laden—he had grown up in Jeddah, and Jeddah was full of people secretly proud of his deeds and his fame. In the palatial home of a Western-educated businessman, I was told that henceforth 9/11 would be like the Kennedy assassination, a contested matter, mysterious, the assailants unknown. The man was young and worldly, his English precise and fluent. I had called on him only months after 9/11; I was made to understand that he came from one of the wealthiest merchant dynasties, and the glitter of his home (bordering on a kind of gaudiness) showed it. Yet he could not let stand the thought that his country had produced this kind of radicalism. The country had opened up to the outsiders only to reveal the rage beneath the surface of harmony and public consent.

The realm was what it was: part *imara* (principality), part religious edifice. A monarch who had styled himself "Custodian of the Two Holy Mosques" was destined to stay close to the religious obscurantists. The religious call had a privileged place in the life of the realm. There were television programs that were given over wholesale to the preachers, religious pages in the daily papers where the scholars of the "religious sciences" expounded on the law and the conduct of the "righteous ancestors" and the requirements of the faith. There was an educational system which favored the religious practitioners—universities and colleges where their writ ran. The men of religion had access to court and to royal favor. The regime and its media—the tedious television programming of the state—covered the visits of the scholars to the senior figures of the dynasty. The coverage, often running without commentary, was meant to convey the unity of the realm. And it conveyed, as well, the ascendancy of the ruler: the members of the *ulama* approaching the king and, depending on their rank and proximity to the ruler, kissing the king's shoulder or nose, offering their allegiance. It was his dominion, and the ritual underlined the primacy of kingship.

There was a message here to the devout, and perhaps to the religious class as well. Rulers could be capricious and could challenge the faith, but these Saudi rulers don't. In neighboring Muslim lands—in Egypt, in Turkey, in Tunisia—the public order had relegated the *ulama* to the sidelines and the religious scholars had not been able to resist the power of the sword and the "reforms" of the state. Arabia was different: the *sharia* was the source of its laws; the religious scholars were everywhere, honored and obeyed. The state deferred to them on the great moral issues—the place of women, conduct in the public space, the very nature of what was *halal* (permissible) and *haram* (impermissible) in personal and public conduct. In return, the religious class acknowledged the primacy of the ruler.

The play between prince and preacher and the willingness to leave the door open to the religious activist is illustrated in the banishment, and then the return to political grace, of a preacher by the name of Ayid al-Qarni. In the late 1980s and early 1990s, Qarni had had his troubles with the rulers. Based in Asir, in the southwest, Qarni had clashed with the powerful governor, Prince Khalid al-Faisal. A son of the late King Faisal, the prince was the undisputed master of this domain. Qarni had gravitated into oppositional politics. He had been pushed to the sidelines and banned from preaching.

In the aftermath of 9/11, Qarni was back in the thick of things. A reporter for the London-based *Al Hayat* sought him out in Riyadh in February 2002, and the result is a long, illuminating interview that casts a floodlight on the terms of engagement between the rulers and the preachers. Qarni was not in the least timid or modest about his calling: he had come back to the field of preaching, he said, to combat the darkness that had descended on the world of Islam, and to do battle against Islam's enemies, to unite the ranks against the "Zionist attacks aimed at the Islamic religion." His return, he let it be known, had come "with the permission of the decision makers and those in authority"—i.e., the rulers. An understanding had been reached, and bygones were bygones. Qarni was keen to set out the terms of the accord he had made with the state and its functionaries. First, there were the teachings of the Quran and the *sunna* (the conduct) of the Prophet, and those were inviolable and beyond discussion. Second, there was national unity that had to be shored up, lest the country be torn asunder: "We have to remember that we were warring tribes until God Almighty brought us together under the banner of the Wahhabi creed." Third, a pledge of obedience was owed the *imam* (the king in this case), which must be honored and observed. In other words, there would be no freelancing this time around. The preachers had their work cut out for them, he added: there were "idle youth" who had taken to new forms of restlessness— blocking traffic in Jeddah, defying the police, harassing women, celebrating Saudi soccer victories with open displays of lawlessness. These youth, said Qarni, had to be called back to the "straight path" and to the ways of the righteous ancestors, and this was a task that only the religious scholars could perform.

Qarni was in the limelight; his passion of the moment was satellite television. He loved the medium and kept count of his television appearances on Al Jazeera, on Abu Dhabi television, on Middle East Broadcasting, etc. He was no hidebound traditionalist, he wanted it known. He noted the shift from the audiocassette tapes of an earlier era to the big, new possibilities opened up by the satellite television channels. A decade earlier, he said, his emphasis was on the "Saudi situation" and its specificity. Now the globe had opened up to him: "When I speak now I imagine that the whole world with all its races and religions is watching me. Our discourse has thus become global, and through it we seek to highlight what men everywhere have in common and to respect the differences among them."

If the discourse has a new "globalizing" tone, the vigilance against "the enemies" remains. The anti-Americanism is never far: "America," he said:

> is an oppressor in the garb of an aggrieved nation. It has used the attacks against itself to prosecute a war that had been decided upon in advance. If we look at the world, and not just the Islamic world, we find that everyone was overjoyed at this attack against America. That was the case in Korea, Japan, and Mexico. . . . The whole world has had its fill with American arrogance and aggression. Perhaps the decision makers in the United States will learn a lesson from these attacks. As for America's war against terror, we don't support it. Instead, we call on America to change its aggressive ways, particularly in the Islamic world, where it has used the veto at the United Nations in favor of Israel more than seventy times.

There was no "clash of civilizations" in the world today, he added. What Saudi Arabia and the Islamic world faced was a campaign against Islam, "carried out by the Jews, spread by Jewish writers, and Jewish publishing houses and institutions. We thank God for this campaign, for it offers proof that we have merited Jewish enmity and suspicion. What is needed are powerful media with credibility and skills, and that the Muslims should rise up together as one man and avoid their internal squabbles at this critical moment."

The peace at home bought with vigilance abroad, and perpetual struggle against the enemies of God and of his people: Qarni was not alone. There was still Safar al-Hawali, imprisoned back in 1994 and released five years later. Imprisonment had not dampened the man's zeal. Less than a month after the terror attacks of 9/11, Hawali turned up with an "open letter" to President George W. Bush. Widely circulated in the country and published abroad in a radical pan-Arabist daily in London, *Al-Quds Al-Arabi*, the letter had the stridency and belligerent self-confidence of the man. This was not the sort of man to apologize for the attack on America or to fault the ideology that spawned the terror. There was pure schadenfreude and no trace of guilt in Hawali's text. And there was no modesty either: Hawali was writing, he said, as an "heir to the righteous Prophet Muhammad, who taught men to speak truth to the mighty and the arrogant in this world so that they may fear God. . . . It is thus that Moses, peace be upon him, spoke to pharaoh, and Jesus, peace upon him, spoke to the Roman governor and to the Chief Rabbi of the temple. I write to you as a member of a community that is persecuted in the same manner that Jesus was persecuted when he faced the aggression of the Jews from one side and of the Romans from the other."

New York was still digging out of the rubble, but Hawali knew only righteousness. "It is regrettable," he wrote, "that America, which had been discovered and peopled by immigrants fleeing persecution, had replaced the Roman Empire in its arrogance and cruelty." For Hawali, Rome is America's true historical predecessor and analogue. In its days of hegemony Rome, too, he wrote, spoke the language of liberty and believed it was the heiress to world culture, Greece's inheritor. On its own terrain, Rome was good to its citizens and blessed with democratic rule and a senate, and the individual Roman was free in his ideology and personal conduct. But Rome had been cruel and arrogant to others. And God sent Rome's way the Vandals from the north, who descended on it and put its civilization to the torch. "It was natural," said Hawali, "that the nations that had suffered at the hands of Rome and endured its might and arrogance were thrilled at Rome's destruction at the hands of these northern barbarians, even though these nations did not know or love these new invaders." The new "American pharaoh" was told to entertain no illusions about the Muslim world and its real feelings toward America and America's grief. "There is no Muslim on the face of the earth who loves and supports you even if he gave blood to your victims, or established intelligence services on your behalf, or authorized you to come up with an educational system for his schools. Anyone who claims to love and support you—and no Muslim can make this claim—has for you the love that a frightened, trapped creature has for its cruel pursuer."

Hawali was speaking to what was playing out in Arab and Muslim streets: the young people were handing out sweets in the West Bank city of Ramallah in celebration of America's grief when Yasser Arafat, in a clear attempt at damage control, turned up at the U.S. consulate in Jerusalem to donate blood for the Americans. In the shadows, the Arab regimes were offering covert help of every kind to the American campaign to hunt down the Islamists. Hawali wanted it known that these rulers were on their own, moved by fear and hypocrisy.

Hawali wanted nothing of the new order in the region that America began to espouse in the aftermath of the terrors of 9/11. "The enemy of liberty can't grant liberty," he said. In Washington there was talk about educational reform in the Arab world, and the Islamists had taken note of that. For this new American bid, Hawali saw only the prospect of sure failure and frustration:

You will say that you aim to remove the sources of hatred and extremism in the sermons and the schools and the media. To that we say, ask what you wish, but be sure that you will not succeed, for our hatred of oppression and love of truth is granted us by our religion, and our Quran, and is mightier than your mountains. Should you persist in your errors, and your intoxication with your might, you will have no choice but to wipe out the Muslims with nuclear and biological weapons, and other means of destruction in your hellish arsenal.

To be sure, Hawali was a true believer willing to risk the wrath of the regime. But there was belligerence in the air. It was hard to draw a line between mainstream jurists and their more radical colleagues. In June 2002, the prayer leader at the Grand Mosque in Mecca, in his *khutba* (Friday sermon), took up the matter of travel and tourism to foreign lands. There were Islamic rules and guidelines, Shaykh Abdulrahman Sudais decreed, to such travel. It had to be to "conservative Islamic lands," for travel to the "swamps of wicked countries" was impermissible. Islam, said this jurist, authorizes travel to "infidel" lands only for the purpose of medical care, work, or study. And for that travel to stay within the bounds of the faith, the traveler had to be "equipped with enough religious faith to ward off temptations, enough knowledge and education to deal with suspicions and with the gaze of non-Muslims." When embarking on such travel, the Muslim had to be on guard: he had to avoid visiting the shrines and tombs of other faiths, he had to stay away from wine and sin. "God Almighty has given our blessed country enough cultural and historical assets to enable people to stay at home and partake of righteous and proper travel." (No small irony: seven years later, in the summer of 2009, Sudais would turn up in London and Birmingham, preaching to several congregations there and urging Muslims in non-Muslim lands to be "ambassadors" for their religion.)

The rulers grew nervous about the wages of religious extremism. They took to calling on the religious scholars and authorities to rein in the extremists. But there was retrogression and belligerence aplenty among those who knew how to stay within the bounds of the religious-political order. On Friday, April 19, 2002, in his *khutba*, the same Shaykh Sudais, whom we already encountered ruling on the dangers of traveling to foreign lands, had let loose on the Jews and Judaism. The Jews, he said, were the "scum of the earth," the "rats of humanity," the "killers of prophets," and the "breakers of promises." The media carried his words. He had the pulpit and the authority. There was a Saudi diplomatic initiative making the rounds. The Crown Prince had been its sponsor. It aimed, we were told, to bridge the gap between Israel and the Arabs. It promised Arab recognition of Israel in return for Israel's withdrawal from the Arab territories occupied in the Six-Day War of 1967. Sudais paid it no heed. The diehards had operated within a permissive environment. They were no isolated band.

The country is opaque, the walls of its privacy are high and prohibitive. There is only so much the *fatwas* of the jurists and the pamphlets of the dissenters can reveal. The closest we are likely to get to a portrait of that time of sedition and trouble is a remarkable work by Abdullah Thabit entitled *The 20th Terrorist (Al-Irhabi 20)*, published in 2006. The author, an educational administrator from the town of Abha, in the mountainous land of Asir, was born in 1973; he had been recruited into the ranks of the diehards as a boy in his early teens. He was to break with them, and his work, a memoir in the convenient guise of a novel, catches that period and the seductions of religious extremism. It took no small amount of courage for this poet and writer to come forth with this chronicle, for the culture frowns on self-revelation of this sort.

The inspiration for this book came of course on 9/11. To Thabit's great surprise, one of the nineteen Arabs who struck America on that day, Ahmed Alnami, came from Thabit's hometown. A horrific event was perilously close to him. "I felt like someone who'd gotten off a boat just in time and watched it capsize with him and the others onboard," Thabit told Faiza Saleh Ambah, a reporter for the *Washington Post*. (See Faiza Saleh Ambah, "The Would-Be Terrorist's Explosive Tell-All Tale," *Washington Post*, July 24, 2006). Had he not jumped, he might have been easily "the 20th terrorist." There was nothing unusual about the beginnings of Thabit's stand-in fictional character, Zahi Al-Jabali. He was born in the countryside around Abha, his family moved to the small city when he was two, he was one of nine children. His family was not particularly privileged, but there was enough to have a decent home—and a television set, which at the time set this family apart from its neighbors. The life of the young boy was mean, his father a veritable tyrant, the physical beatings at home and school a source of great misery. He tended his father's goats in his spare time and did an unusual amount of reading. He was good at school, and this brought him to the attention of the religious extremists. The hook was soccer.

He loved the sport, and the recruiters on the lookout for new adherents to their ideology used it to draw him into their web. His family had wanted nothing to do with politics. A generation earlier, an older brother of his had been on the fringe of Juhayman al-Utaybi's band of zealots. The forces of order had let him go, but the panic of that time had remained with this family.

But some doors are made to be broken, not opened, the narrator says in *The 20th Terrorist*. The young boy was now willing to defy his parents. There was the companionship of soccer camps, and there was steady religious indoctrination. He came to despise his family members; he wanted them to rid themselves of their television set, to remove the photographs in the household, to banish music—much beloved in Asir. He told his father that he was robbing the family of its share in paradise. He took on the habits of the *jamaa* (the group). He donned a shin-length *thoub*, he grew a long beard, he mimicked the affectations of the group. "We learned that ours is a world of unbelievers," he said. "We were the band of the saved, all the others were condemned." He wondered how his group and its leaders financed its activities; he learned that they did it through theft, and that theft from the state in the interest of jihad was pleasing to Allah. By 1990, when Saddam Hussein swept into Kuwait, the boy of seventeen had become something of an enforcer in his own right. He bullied his schoolmates, frightened the more timid of the teachers. When a teacher gave an assignment that asked for an essay on a preferred television program, he warned the teacher that he was leading his students to damnation and ruin. The *jamaa* had power in the school. The more attractive of the boys sought the *jamaa*'s protection to ward off the sexual predators who stalked them. The *jamaa* decreed that it was permissible to cheat on English examinations because English was the language of the infidels. Even the English teacher was embarrassed about the subject he was teaching. In the bigger world beyond the school, this was the time of the "killer *fatwas*" and of the ideological war that the preachers had launched against the Saudi state.

A chance came the narrator's way to go to Afghanistan. He decided against it; it was not the time to become a mujahid. His alienation from his family had grown extreme. A year would pass without him sharing their food, riding in their cars. He became something of a freelance preacher, giving Friday sermons in mosques in neighboring villages. This is a rainy part of the country with deep wadis, and often he would go out in the rain, bareheaded for hours at a time. He tells of a truly bizarre ritual that an older companion introduced him to. The two of them would make weekly excursions to the cemetery. They would lie down for hours in open graves while listening to sermons played on the car's cassette player that warned of the terrible fate that lay in store for the apostates and the unbelievers.

There remained something in young Zahi that helped rescue him. There was still deep within him a love of music and of poetry. Jealousies and suspicions played a part, too, in his break with the group that came when he was twenty. Younger boys had been drawn to him, and others in the *jamaa* were circulating rumors about sexual relations with the youngsters. He had grown weary of the bigotry, he says. He enrolled in university, in Arabic literature. He rediscovered his love of the poem and the song and of sports. His family bought him a car, and this gave him freedom to roam about and to be on his own. On the way to the world out of the zealot's grip, he was given a savage beating by members of the *jamaa* who had lured him into the mountains on the promise of a "dialogue" with his former companions.

Zahi Al-Jabali heals. He graduates from the university, becomes a teacher, publishes his poetry, comes into fame in Abha and its surroundings. In the spring of 2001, he publishes an essay on the beauty of music, and on the follies of those who keep it out of the educational curriculum. Thirty religious scholars ask the preeminent leader of the tribe to which Abdullah belongs to bring the "apostate" to heel. His own father denounces him; the father is told that his son is declaring *halal* what is proscribed by God—and in a secular newspaper. Before a larger assembly, an influential cleric beseeches God to bring about Zahi's ruin, to "freeze the blood in his veins," to make of him, and of secularists like him, a lesson in this world and in the hereafter, to make widows of their wives and orphans of their children. Help comes from the emir of the province, a poet, painter, and patron of culture and of the arts. For two whole months, the narrator tells us, he went around with a pistol in the pocket of his *thoub*.

It is Tuesday, September 11, 2001, the planes crashing into the Twin Towers. He couldn't believe it, he couldn't believe that young men from his country—and Ahmed Alnami from his hometown, a face familiar to him—had pulled off that catastrophic deed. Now he wanted vindication, an apology, an acknowledgment that he had spotted the troubles early. It was a "bitter victory," he adds. "My country was seared by a fire she had not bothered to put out before." The small world he knew, the training camps he had been part of a few years earlier, had become part of a big story.

CHAPTER THREE

Homeward Bound

On May 12, 2003, the chickens came home to roost. Three bombings in Riyadh brought home the wages of religious radicalism. Three housing compounds were targeted by terrorists. Thirty-four people were killed, including eight Americans, two Britons, and nine of the assailants. It was immediately proclaimed that this was Saudi Arabia's 9/11. The Saudis had held themselves apart from the terror that had struck American shores. They had insisted that 9/11 was no affair of theirs. They had explained away the "death pilots" and the Saudi prisoners at Guantánamo. No less than twenty-five percent of these prisoners, rounded up in the aftermath of the terror attacks, came from Saudi Arabia. But there had been a closing of the ranks. Those were "innocent boys" who had been unjustly imprisoned, idealistic and pious youth who had made their way to Pakistan and Afghanistan to fight for the faith: philanthropic and charitable work had taken them to these lands, and a blindly indiscriminate American policy had rounded them up as part of a campaign to smear Arabia's reputation. Now, with the attacks on Riyadh, there was a sudden break with the official line. This was not remote Bali (the scene of the bombing some seven months earlier which had targeted Western, principally Australian, visitors to that once tranquil paradise) or a tourist site in Egypt, nor was this an assault in infidel lands.

A different sentiment now took hold. The secretive realm that had insisted on its innocence was willing to do things it had hitherto resisted. The U.S. Treasury Department had been pressing for access to the country's banking system and to the workings of Saudi charities. It had been difficult to enlist Saudi help. In their fashion, in 2002, the Saudis had promised that a commission would be established and given the powers of oversight of the country's charities. Those charities numbered in the hundreds, by one estimate close to five hundred organizations of varying reach and size. Nothing had come of that commission. Now a new pledge was made that the Saudis would do better. A team of Internal Revenue Service and FBI agents, it was announced, would be stationed in Arabia. The country's finances would be made more transparent and the charities would be directed to focus their work, and their wealth, on the problems of Arabia itself. There was growing poverty in the realm, and the rulers were now willing to own up to this fact.

Breaking with custom (and pride), the Crown Prince had begun to visit impoverished neighborhoods in the capital, accompanied by reporters, promising that "reform" and help were on the way. The self-image of a prosperous country at peace had to be set aside. As the state hunted down the conspirators, the preachers went to work, and a full-scale assault began against the *ghulat* (extremists). The very nature of the faith was being redefined away from excessive zeal and from the jihadists.

Within days of the Riyadh attacks, forty-seven members of the country's *ulama* issued what must be reckoned as one of the principal political-religious documents to come out of that country. The signatories included establishment, quietist jurists, but there were also dissidents familiar to us by now: there were the firebrands Safar al-Hawali and Salman al-Awda; there was Ayid al-Qarni, now rehabilitated and playing by the rules. There was an older scholar who had straddled the fence between the rulers and the religious radicals: Abdullah ibn Jibrin, now retired but still a figure of genuine standing among the diehards and the purists. The religious-scholarly establishment was rallying around the regime. A compromise had been struck and a price had been paid for the consent and the support of the radicals.

The text opens with an unequivocal denunciation of the deed: "We condemn the bombings which took place in Riyadh, and we affirm their impermissibility and state that they are counter to the *sharia*. Any discussion of this deed must proceed from a candid denunciation of it, with no ambiguity whatsoever in the face of a deed at once shameful and prohibited. This country is a refuge for Muslims. The jurists have decreed that the blood of anyone who entered a Muslim country and was granted a pledge of safety cannot be shed, even if that pledge was in violation of the principles of the *sharia*." Eight Americans had been killed in these attacks; the jurists had ruled that the presence of those Americans in the land had been at the invitation of the rulers. The larger question of whether "infidels" should enter Arabia was sidestepped. It was enough for now to acknowledge that foreigners who had been given safe passage by the authorities had been betrayed and murdered.

A number of the signatories had given explicit *fatwas* in support of jihad; now the jihad had to be theologically fenced in. Jihad is a duty, to be sure, these men ruled. But it has its "principles and conditions." The resort to bloodletting is particularly strict in "Quranic texts, in the *hadiths* (sayings) of the Prophet, and in the severe punishment held out to those who violate its strictures and commit aggression." The signatories found ample rulings in the Quran to sustain their view. There was God's word: "He who kills a believer by design shall burn in hell forever. He shall incur the wrath of Allah, who will lay His curse on him and prepare him for a woeful scourge" (4:93). And there was another verse cited by the jurists: "Whoever killed a human being, except as a punishment for murder or wicked crimes, shall be looked upon as though he had killed all human-kind; and that whoever saved a human life shall be regarded as though he had saved all mankind" (5:32).

This was a land of many nationalities and faiths and creeds and sects, these men of religion observed. The "enemies of Islam" were keeping watch; they were eager to wage war against the Muslims, and this sort of sedition was likely to give them the perfect cover. "Nor do good intentions acquit wrongful deeds. Love of religion cannot take precedence over the *sharia*." In other words, the zeal that had once acquitted young jihadists was no longer acceptable. The jurists looked to the *sira* (conduct) of the Prophet Muhammad and found ample precedent for prudence. After quitting his native Mecca, the Prophet had bided his time in Medina: it had taken him thirteen years, these men noted, to authorize a military campaign against Mecca. Faith can't be unbridled; the world imposes its limits and restraints. And this

Saudi realm, in particular, was to be off limits to those who would commit violent deeds. "We note the danger of bringing war and terror inside this country, for it is the fortress of Islam and the home of its revelation. We ask that the *ulama*, and the seekers of religious knowledge, should be aware of this, and should speak out against the sowing of dissension."

The order, and the rulers, had been given their due. But the signatories still saved some of their fire and ammunition for the United States. "It is important that this episode not be used by the Americans as a pretext for their own designs against the educational system, and the judiciary, and the laws of this land." The educational system in the country was sound; it had schooled all the literate people in the country "without spreading evil." It was in the nature of the Bush administration and of "some extremists in its ranks" to try to use this crisis to penetrate Saudi Arabia, to shut down its charities and religious institutions. A line had to be drawn for the Americans, and for those secularists within, who might have their own schemes and accounts to settle. Terror was one thing, but the integrity of the educational system of the country was beyond reproach and beyond the scrutiny of outsiders. Opposition to America, these men opined, was not the "monopoly of a religious country like Saudi Arabia, or of other Arab and Islamic lands. Hatred for the evil policies of America is growing in all corners of the world. There is an additional hatred in the Muslim world only because the Islamic world is targeted in its religion and culture and wealth and way of life, as it is easy to see."

There was a manhunt for the plotters who planned the bombings and the preachers who had lent their support.

Nineteen men were being sought by the authorities. The terrorists were now beyond the pale. This realm that dreads naming and acknowledging troubles now had to admit that there were indeed "sleeper cells" in that country, that some of its own people had taken up arms against the state. There were armed clashes in Riyadh, terrorists with rocket launchers slugging it out with the forces of order in the capital. There were clashes in the holy city of Mecca between the police and armed bands of zealots. Denial had run its course, and the theological arguments against the terrorists grew increasingly emphatic. "He who would brand another man an unbeliever will have his own words rebound on him," the head of the judiciary in the country, Shaykh Saleh al-Luhaidan, declared in mid-August 2003. It is important to think well of one's fellow man, "to forgive those who err." There were people out there, he warned, claiming the mantle of religious scholarship and authority without possessing the qualifications and the temperament to do so. There were "external and internal conspiracies" that would divide "the flock from its leaders" and the "Muslim community from its *ulama*."

It was a moment of peril: order and obedience were now uppermost. In the same vein, one of the luminaries of the religious establishment, the minister of Islamic affairs, openly said that "excess in religious piety" was a form of sedition, a pernicious attack on the faith. A circle had been closed, a return to Wahhabism's emphasis on the need for the ruler's protection and the knowledge that religious faith must be anchored in a public order and a ruler's embrace. Within three months of the May 12 attacks, the state owned up to the extent of religious radicalism. It announced that seven hundred clerics had been removed from their posts and more than a thousand preachers had been banned from delivering sermons and leading prayers in the mosques. The radicalism had drawn on a vast apparatus and had become entrenched in the religious and educational system in the land.

Only a handful of religious scholars remained outside this consensus. Three of them in particular held on: Nasser al-Fahd, a young religious scholar from Riyadh, a diehard with uncompromising views who had served a three-year prison sentence in the mid-1990s; Ali al-Khudeir, also of Riyadh, who had issued a *fatwa* authorizing war under "the banner of the tyrant Saddam Hussein against the Crusaders"; and a Kuwaiti-born preacher, Ahmad al-Khalidi, who had left his country in his mid-twenties in 1993 to make his home in Saudi Arabia. For these three, the battle continued. They issued a common *fatwa* in support of the nineteen fugitives implicated in the Riyadh bombings. They declared them mujahidin, holy warriors. They declared impermissible, *haram,* "informing on them, or harming their reputation, or rendering any form of assistance against them." Furthermore, they declared *kafir* anyone who aided the war against the Taliban. And they wrote off as a form of heresy the work of Muslims who engaged in science, medicine, or mathematics. In more tranquil times, the opinions of these extremists may have been ignored. But it was a time of peril, and the rulers were determined to show that no mercy would be granted those who endanger the realm. The three men were sent to prison.

In June 2003, a young merchant in his late thirties, educated at one of the great private universities in the United States, wrote to me an anguished letter about the state of U.S.-Saudi relations. A month earlier, I had talked with him late into the night in Jeddah about the mood of his country, and about the spreading influence of this new Islamism and the "orphaned" modernity. He was to return to these themes in his letter: "I see a great burden to fix U.S.-Arab relations in turbulent times—I feel there is a voice not being heard today in America. There are people here genuinely keen to see Arabia move into the modern age—but require an interested audience (the United States) and, more importantly, the vehicle to get there. I owe it to the country that provided me the finest education and worldly experience to shed light and perspectives on this current conflict lest we do disservice to that old bond."

A year or so earlier, this young man and his Jeddah-born (and also American-educated) wife had been kind enough to receive me and my wife in their home. They had invited another couple of the same generation and outlook. And we were joined, as well, by a brother of our host, a refined man, a psychologist with a deep interest in Christianity and in the educational theories of John Dewey. It was the kind of evening you travel for. There was candor, a lack of any dissimulation. And like practically all evenings there, it lasted well into the night. There was to the evening a touch of the Levant: it was the town (Jeddah) and this class of young people formed by their own land, but by America and by Beirut as well. Our hostess was a young woman of flair and assertiveness. She was a woman of this city, she wanted it known. Her university education had taken her to the United States. But she had been made ready for that passage by her early schooling in Jeddah. That was a different era, she lamented, and more open. There was less emphasis on religion and religious subjects, and there was in the land a genuine desire for the modern world, a curiosity about the movies of Egypt and about the literary output of Beirut, about the pop culture of America.

All this has been wrecked, she said. She had two young boys of school age; she had pulled all sorts of strings to get them into a private international school. She dreaded the prospect of their return to the government school system and the knowledge that would be transmitted to them were they to be forced back into that system. She spoke nostalgically of the Jeddah of her childhood and of the promise of change in the air. There had been realism, she insisted. It was known that the country placed its own limits on social and cultural mores, but there was optimism and a sense that the modern push had become irresistible. Now the country had taken a different turn, and this immensely articulate woman dreaded what lay in store for them all.

A sense of superiority, she noted, had come with this piety: an insistence that this land and its ways were infallible, that other lands and peoples were fallen or depraved or lived in error. It was new, this feeling of perfection. Again she returned to a comparison with what had been the norm in the years of her schooling. She and her peers had not been given this sense of separateness from other nations and other religions. Now that belief had been sharpened, and driven into the young. There were these perfectly respectable jurists preaching the folly of traveling to foreign lands and mixing with infidels, calling on Saudis to hold themselves aloof from other nations. There was Arabia's true way and there were the ways of others. Jews and Nasranis (Christians) and even Muslim secularists were to be avoided. One could not greet them, share their joys and sorrows.

For all this despondency, these men and women were not about to pack up and leave. One couple had quit the country for Europe, only to return. They had means and the skills for a good life in London, but they could not conceive of a normal life beyond their extended families. Moreover, they had done well by the system and they had no trouble admitting it. What was discernible among them was a strong sense of political disinheritance. They had made their peace with their political lot—they couldn't rule, they would always come into the courts of princes reconciled to the hegemony of Al Saud. Once upon a time, in the 1950s and 1960s, their fathers and skilled men like them had had a sense of place: their skills and modern education had given them real functions in the building of a more modern Arabia. They had been favored by the dynasty and they could see the possibility of breaking the back of the religious obscurantism. But the new religious breed now had the upper hand, and those zealots had no regard for what had been accomplished in the past.

It was not so much the prospect of revolution that troubled young people of skills and education, but the grinding down of the modern edifice, the drawing down of the country's assets, the infrastructure and the modern will overwhelmed by the numbers and by the anger all around. In their despairing vision, the state would no longer defend modern ideals and practice;

it would continue to give ground to the religious reactionaries. They and their like would have no choice but to submit to the logic of things or to pack up and leave.

I could not see this group of men and women, and their peers, winning a test of wills against the vigilantes and the zealots. They knew their political and cultural weakness. The erosion of the Saudi-American relationship was a nightmare to this class. So long as the shadow of American power hung over the land, they felt a measure of security and confidence. America had helped midwife the modern Saudi world. Saudi Arabia had slipped into the American orbit. The American presence had given my hosts, and thousands like them, a vital connection, perhaps some political shelter and cover.

The American presence was under attack; the American embassy in the Diplomatic Quarter in Riyadh—it was once in the relative tumult of Jeddah, along with other embassies—was a gilded cage in a silent, remote part of the city. The police kept track of the comings and goings of Saudis who ventured into the Diplomatic Quarter, and the Americans who broke out of compound life were few and far between. There was only so much a foreign power could see and could really know about a country with a fierce sense of privacy and reserve.

America could not win the battle of modernity for the besieged liberals. The despairing note of my young Saudi correspondent who had written to me about the state of U.S.-Saudi relations had something of that desire written into it. At any rate, the royals monopolized that strategic relationship. It was they who granted military facilities and air space for the Americans, and oil discounts. In the main, it was they who knew the details and the subtleties of that relationship. There was little traffic between these two societies that escaped the control of the Saudi state.

Nor was this liberal class itself immune to the call of anti-Americanism. Our hostess in Jeddah gave away the dilemma of the modernists. At one point in our discussions, she sensed that I had wanted some acknowledgment of what had befallen America in the terror attacks of 9/11. She would not provide it. "We have no power in this land," she said, "and where there is no power, there is no responsibility." In this young woman's reckoning, the American presence and its terms were negotiated by the House of Saud. She was not a party to the terms of that encounter. She knew that young men from her country had flown into the Twin Towers in New York and had crashed into the Pentagon; she was not one to partake of the nihilistic denial given voice by large numbers of Arabs who refused to accept that nineteen young men of their own had committed those horrific crimes. She knew that a wealthy heir to a construction dynasty from her own city, Osama bin Laden, five or six years older than herself and her husband, was at the center of a terror campaign of global reach. But the political powerlessness offered her a measure of absolution from all that.

These modernists knew the cunning of the diehards and the chameleon ways of their sympathizers. And in the privacy of their intimate gatherings, they could, with reasonable confidence, name the businessmen who hedged their bets by feeding and financing the forces of terror. They themselves were paying dearly for the spreading influence of this cultural radicalism. But their ways were what they were, and the anti-Americanism was the reflexive response of other-wise intelligent and educated people who bristled at their own political weakness but could do nothing about it. They claimed that they savored the American message but hacked away at the messenger.

This was a battle this class could not win. They could never be more anti-American than the diehards; they could not outdo the militant traditionalists in their aversion to Israel and Zionism. The temptations of anti-Americanism, and anti-modernism, were too strong to resist. These modernists could not let well enough alone. They hailed the suicide bombers in Jerusalem without realizing that the ruin would spread from the streets of Jerusalem to the compounds of Riyadh.

It was only when the terror hit Riyadh in May 2003 that a handful of brave commentators drew a line, and drew the proper conclusions: if you bless violence and its perpetra-tors in Jerusalem and New York, they are sure to turn up at your doorstep in Riyadh. Here is an enlightened and brave columnist, Jamal Khashoggi, once a columnist for the Jeddah-based *Arab News,* making the same point forthrightly in the Arabic daily *Al-Watan* after the terror attacks in Riyadh: "We have made the same mistake that many cultures do when they tolerate fanatics. Now, thank God, we have awakened." More directly still, the editors of *Arab News* were able to see after the attacks of Riyadh the price of winking at terror abroad: "Those who gloat over September 11, those who happily sup-port suicide bombings in Israel and Russia, those who con-sider non-Muslims less human than Muslims and therefore somehow disposable, all bear part of the responsibility for the

Riyadh bombs. We cannot say that suicide bombings in Israel and Russia are acceptable but not in Saudi Arabia. The cult of suicide bombings has to stop."

For this culture and its permissible ways of expression, for its tendency to close ranks and to leave things unnamed and unacknowledged, this introspection was a remarkable break with routine. The specter of "Talibanization" threatened the society, yet another journalist of *Al-Watan* wrote:

> Though few would publicly admit it, Saudis have become hostages of the backward agenda of Bin Laden supporters who in effect have hijacked our society. Progressive voices have been silenced. The religious and social oppression of women means that half the population is forced to stay behind locked doors. Members of the religious police harass us in public spaces, and sometimes even in our homes, about our clothing and haircuts. A civil war is raging, one we have long pretended does not exist.

The writer, Sulaiman al-Hattlan, was speaking for a wing of the society that had seen the steady erosion of its rights. The modernists had found a measure of daring. (There were limits to the new openness. Khashoggi lost his editorship of *Al-Watan* over what was deemed an unacceptable cartoon: a sketch of a member of the religious police with a belt of explosives, and the word *fatwa* scrawled across the belt. The senior clerics in the realm weighed in, and the man was pushed out from the helm of a paper which he had turned into a relatively open, and brave, forum of expression. After a decent interval, he returned to his job.)

In truth, the modernists had been sowing the wind. In April 2002, Ghazi Algosaibi, a luminary of this class of Saudis, provoked a storm in the United Kingdom, where he was serving as his country's ambassador. He published a poem in the London-based *Al Hayat* in praise of a Palestinian bomber, a young woman who had killed herself and two Israelis at a supermarket in Jerusalem a fortnight earlier. Algosaibi was a self-styled poet and gadfly who had held several cabinet portfolios and an earlier ambassadorial appointment to Bahrain. He was heir and beneficiary to the best his country had to offer. Born in 1940, he hailed from an influential merchant family from Bahrain. An island people with exposure to the wider world, the Algosaibis had been agents and representatives of the legendary Ibn Saud in the years of conquest and royal consolidation. When Arabia was still battling its way through poverty and illiteracy, Ghazi Algosaibi had been given the chance to study in Cairo, then Southern California, capping it with a doctorate from England.

Algosaibi handed his country's diplomacy a full-blown crisis with his elegy to the young bomber, Ayat Akhras. He praised her as a "bride of loftiness," and saw in her cruel and violent end a contrast to the impotence and supplication of the Arabs. To her and other suicide bombers, he paid tribute, acknowledging a debt owed them:

> May God and the prophets and the holy men be my
>   witnesses, you are martyrs
> You died to honor God's word in lands where the dearest
>   are prisoners
> You committed suicide? It is we who committed suicide in a
>   world of the living dead

We have grown so impotent until impotence grew weary of us
We have wept until weeping disdained us
We pleaded and complained to the tyrant of the White
    House whose heart was full of blackness
Tell Ayat, the bride of loftiness, that when the mighty men,
    the pride of my people, grow impotent, a beautiful
    woman embraces death with a smile while the leaders
    are running away from death
Doors of heaven are open for her
Tell those who compose *fatwas* to tread carefully, perhaps
    there are *fatwas* that the heavens disdain
When jihad calls, the ink will go silent, and the jurists
There is no plebiscite of *fatwas* when jihad calls, on the day
    of jihad it is blood that calls.

There were religious scholars and jurists who had taken a jaundiced view of suicide operations; indeed, a high-ranking member of the Saudi religious establishment had been forthright enough to say that such suicide/homicide operations were in violation of Islam. Algosaibi had upped the ante—he had outflanked those who render *fatwas* and religious edicts; the man of diplomacy and of the state exalting blood and terror. This was chic, and among the Arabs of London it had an audience. The ambassador of a country within the American orbit writing of a White House with a black heart and a tyrannical master—the crowd loved this, and Algosaibi was not above catering to the dark instincts of the crowd.

Algosaibi had found the perfect vehicle. The London-based *Al Hayat*, owned by a member of the House of Saud, Khalid bin Sultan (a son of the defense minister), was staffed by Arab nationalists; the Arab intellectuals in Europe and the United

States loved it and filled its columns with the pieties and fidelities of Arab nationalism. Algosaibi was on favorable terrain, and he gloried in the attention. He could never fully grasp and accept that a price is paid for this fling with extremism: the fire would rage, he was sure, in Jerusalem and would never engulf his land. "It is poetry," said the assistant editor of *Al Hayat*, Ghassan Charbel, in praise of the poem. "There is strong feeling in the Arab street that is reflected in this piece." The street rules, and its furies exempt and ennoble even all ruinous and terrible things.

In the months that followed, Algosaibi would be relieved of his diplomatic post and dispatched back home. But he came back to a cabinet appointment as minister of water. A second appointment, as minister of labor, would follow. To judge by an account that surfaced in the press in mid-January 2003, Algosaibi was unrepentant, and an educated audience at a cultural festival in Riyadh gave him a hero's welcome. "Don't applaud," he quipped, "lest they expel you from London." For this audience and this speaker, the morality—let alone the practicality—of suicide bombings was not to be questioned.

In a twist of irony, a group of Palestinian intellectuals in the West Bank and Gaza, led by Sari Nusseibah, scion of a noted Jerusalem family and a political philosopher and educator of genuine moderation, had opened a searching debate about the entire phenomenon of suicide/homicide bombings and about the damage they had done to Palestinian political culture. It was easier for Algosaibi. He was feeding distant fires. That very evening in Riyadh, he was still exalting the young boys and young women of terror redeeming the Arab world with a "river of blood." He called up the memory of the great Muslim warrior

Saladin: were that warrior to turn up amidst the Arabs again, he would throw himself into his grave covered up with shame. "It is my dream to cut down the dove of peace and to replace it with a falcon that would slay this fear."

There is no record of what Algosaibi said four months later when the terrors hit Riyadh, whether he offered a view of what had descended on the capital of his country. Given his love of the limelight, and the genuine sense of shock that overtook the Saudi political elite and public, it would be safe to assume that he must have had some choice words for the plotters and those who aided and abetted them. It would be safe to assume, as well, that the man could see no connection between the terror he hailed in Jerusalem and the terror he condemned in Arabia. It was enough for him to rail against the Americans and to proclaim a holy struggle against Israel. The age of restraint and introspection had not dawned. An elite that would turn away from the temptations of extremism had not yet stepped forth to accept the possibilities, and the discipline, of modernity.

The terror would not subside: the stubborn assertion that there were no "sleeper cells" in the country would be shown for the idle and self-defeating boast it was. On the night of November 8–9, 2003, during the holy month of Ramadan, the terrorists struck again. This time, they chose a housing compound in Riyadh within proximity of the Diplomatic Quarter. This compound's residents were almost entirely Arab and Muslim expatriates, Lebanese and Egyptians in particular. Gunmen had struck first, then a booby-trapped car full of explosives was driven into the compound: nearly 120 people were wounded in the attack, and seventeen were killed. The minister of interior, the monarch's full brother, Prince Naif bin Abdulaziz, turned up at the scene. He vowed swift retribution against the perpetrators.

To judge by the regime's public response, and by the way the Saudi press covered the episode, a choice was made by the custodians of the regime to take to the airwaves and to work with what the terrorists had wrought. Gone was the old formula of ducking for cover and hoping that the troubles would go away. There were the grim tales of what had befallen simple Egyptian families; there was the story of a bride from Lebanon cut down in her prime. There were "human interest" stories about the men of the police so devoted to the work of rescue that residents of the compound brought them their Ramadan pre-dawn meal, because the police had worked through the night. Here was proof, the men of the regime said over and over again, that Saudi Arabia was stalked by indiscriminate terror that struck Muslims and non-Muslims alike.

By now we were in a familiar world: the theological and political arguments were an echo of what had played out in the aftermath of the terror attacks that had hit Riyadh six months earlier. There was a new twist to the story, though, that laid bare the play between the religious diehards and the secularists. The radical preacher Safar al-Hawali came forth with an odd and transparent offer. He would mediate between the regime and the terrorists, he said. He would help cap the volcano and use his authority with the militants. The price, he let it be known, would be deeper concessions to the religious current, a rollback of some of the reform measures that had been introduced into public life, an olive branch to the militants, the promise from the authorities of good treatment for those on the run. In other words, there would be peace for the authorities in return for a bargain between the rulers and the Islamists.

Hawali's message was not subtle; the terror had sprung from the "deviations" and the compromises and the backsliding in public life. Only a return to the rigors of the faith, and a rupture of the alliances with "infidel" powers, would bring about social peace and the acquiescence of the disaffected youth. There was a diplomatic initiative that the Crown Prince had put forth in 2002 for accommodation between Israel and the Palestinians: it was moribund, but it would have to be scrapped nonetheless. There was girls' education: it once had been a monopoly of the religious enforcers but had been taken away from them; the old system would have to be restored. Some committees were looking into the textbooks and trying to strip them of passages of intolerance of Westerners and other Muslim (non-Wahhabi) sects; those committees would have to be disbanded. "Peace" could be bought at the price of greater social and cultural retrogression.

Those eager to keep the religious reactionaries at bay could only marvel at Hawali's proposal. "Saudis are among the most religiously devout and observant in the world," observed Mashari al-Thaydi, a writer for *Asharq Al-Awsat* and a journalist noted for his courage in the face of the obscurantists. "They are in no need of those who would call for more rigorous enforcement of the faith. What the Saudis need is a full-scale plan for social development and political and economic reform." It is their life in this world, he added, that required repair. Those Islamists had wanted nothing less than a monopoly over the domestic and foreign policy choices of the country.

For the rulers, the choice was starkly put. As they hunted down the terrorists, they gave an initial response to Hawali and his like: there would be no dialogue with the terrorists. The answer would come, they said, from "the rifle and the sword." They were sure, it seemed, that a society that had seen and experienced the wages of terror would grant them a warrant for a wider crackdown on a radicalism more deeply entrenched in their land than they had been willing to admit. This religious radicalism was blowing through a country possessed of considerable wealth. These religious agitators were not at work in the caves of Afghanistan, or the slums of Cairo and Karachi. Amid the second thoughts, one of the militants, Ali al-Khudeir, came forth with a declaration of repentance. Typically, this was the "new" religion, and its ways: the declaration was made in a television interview with one of the "born again" moderates, Ayid al-Qarni. Khudeir had been one of the holdouts; he had issued *fatwas* in favor of Saddam Hussein, he had ruled against informing on the terror cells in Arabia. In the debate in his country, his had been a particularly merciless voice: he had declared *kuffar* a number of Saudi intellectuals of secular leanings. He had been in error, Khudeir declared on Saudi state television. The terror attack in Riyadh some days earlier changed him, he said. He "wept" for the children and the women who had perished in that attack. Those who had done that deed had been carried away by excessive zeal.

He had done ideological battle against the state; that, too, was wrong: "The state is a Muslim state, its *ulama* are Muslims." He had authorized attacks against "infidels" living in Arabia, but he would do so no more. Those in Arabia with valid permits granted them by the rulers were off limits: they were given a pledge of safety, and their "blood and property" are impermissible. There was no "apostasy" in Arabia, Khudeir now proclaimed. There was religious observance everywhere, all the obligations of Islam were fulfilled, and one can't attribute apostasy to a society of this kind. Nor was it permissible, he added, to take up arms against the police, which he had authorized as well in another *fatwa*. "I now realize that the *fatwa* is wrong, and I completely disassociate myself from it. . . . The police and the men of the army are Muslims, and it is forbidden to war against them."

The practice of the Islamists permits a measure of dissimulation in the face of adversity and difficult odds. There was no way of knowing whether Khudeir was sincere in what he said. He was, it should be noted, in prison when he made his statement of repentance. But his retreat was astounding for its repudiation of practically everything he had stood for. He no longer sought war with the Jews and the Christians, he said. If these people entered "the lands of Islam" for a legitimate goal, then war against them is prohibited, for there is in their presence a "benefit for the Muslims." The jihad remains, Khudeir said, but only the powers that be, the ruler to be exact, can authorize it. Young men now seeking jihad in Iraq were advised to stay away from Iraq, for it had become a land of "sedition" and war.

Ayid al-Qarni became a Pied Piper of this new mood of repentance and reconciliation. In January 2004, with these media breakthroughs behind him, he now saw merit in the right of women to drive their cars. He hedged his bets: this was the best of a bad lot, he said, and his opinion should be taken as a statement of personal preference. On balance, he observed, were he to choose between a woman driving her own car or "being alone with a foreign driver," he would take the first option. Were his own daughters and sisters to ask for this right, he would probably not grant it to them, he added, but it was important to take up this controversial public issue, to distinguish between "fundamental" and "marginal" things. For himself, he wanted it known that he was a man of "dialogue," interested in raising new, urgent questions. "Saudi society," he added, in a rare display of introspection, was a "hard society that only accepts the truth of a singular line of thinking. He who disagrees with us is deemed to be in error, while we are always and invariably, in our view, in the right. In this age, it is important to acknowledge that there are other opinions that have to be heard."

Qarni's days of freelancing were clearly behind him. He was a poster child now of the new "moderation." There were jihadists on the run, and he issued a public appeal to them yet again to lay down their arms, to honor the obedience they owed to the authority of their elders and of the rulers. It was idle to go underground, he said; it was better to turn back to the "straight path" and to have faith in the mercy of those in authority. If zeal and good intentions and ignorance of the truths and strictures of the faith had led these militants astray, the door was open to those who would return to the fold.

Amid this critical time of trouble, in early January 2004, there was a big media spectacle staged by the authorities: Saudi television broadcast the taped confessions of twenty-nine people who had been rounded up by the police from the ranks of the armed militants. The names of the men were not released, nor were their faces shown on the television screen. The privacy given them was a display of the ruling order's discretion, part of the social pact between the rulers and the families and clans from which these militants hailed. The officials of the Ministry of Interior who oversaw these confessions knew, of course, that the strategy carried with it the risk that the whole thing would be dismissed as a stage-managed affair. But that was a risk they were willing to take.

The penitent is always a witness to an orthodoxy's self-image. In a society heavy with censorship and self-censorship, access to the airwaves is jealously guarded and a rebel's testimony is intended to buttress the reigning truth. The theme underlined again and again by the official truth is that of innocence led astray, of "ignorance" of the "true religion" leading young men down the path to sedition and ruin. Here is "Terror Cell Member Number 1" on how the evildoers worked their will on the gullible:

> They take advantage of the ignorance of the young, they give them *hadiths* and religious proofs and they twist these sources to their desires. . . . They come to you with strange utterances, tell you what to do. In return for what? In return for paradise, they said. This was the exchange, for the promise of paradise you had to use explosives in Saudi Arabia, slaughter this or that man or that particular king or attack the Americans. They told us that they wanted to build an Islamic state, and carry out the instructions of the Prophet, peace be upon him, of banishing the infidels from the Arabian Peninsula.

"Member Number 3" spoke of the incitement of recruiters who knew holy warfare and combat: "They brought me two men they called mujahidin who had been in Afghanistan. They told me about jihad and raids in Afghanistan, about the good merit earned by those who partake of jihad."

The idea that the sedition was bred on foreign shores, away from the faith and the consensus of Arabia, is dear to the rulers and their allies in the scholarly-judicial establishment. And "Member Number 11" gave evidence of that contagion from foreign sources. "Imported *fatwas* were coming from outside, over the internet, urging combat and struggle against the tyrants, for to these preaching these foreign *fatwas* the Saudi government had become a tyranny." The next testimonial, that of "Member Number 12," is meant to convey the guile of the recruiters who begin with religious matters and then inevitably end up with political sedition. This is what he said of the man who had pulled him into the net: "When I met him he always talked about jihad and about coming to the aid of Muslims. He then took the number of my mobile telephone; he sent me messages about jihad. At the beginning he never talked about *takfir* (declaring others apostates) or about the impermissibility of modern sciences. After he saw my increasing receptivity to him, he began maligning the state. He ended up declaring it a state of unbelief and apostasy."

For the custodians of religious and political power, the cure to all this sedition, this confusion in the realm, is of course a proper knowledge of the faith, deeper study of it. And "Member Number 26" confirms this reasoning: "Saudi youth is most easily reached and influenced by religion, and through the religious message. This is due to two factors: the dearth of religious knowledge in the Saudi street, and the fact that the *ulama* have not engaged in a proper confrontation with the sources of trouble."

What begins with religion ends with politics: the target of all these religious messages, the rulers were keen to underline, is the order of the kingdom. "Member Number 27" makes the state's case: "They only talk about the Saudi rulers; they all talk about the *ulama* of the Saudi state. All their effort is concentrated against the Saudi state." God and God's religion had been made a party to the naked ambitions of men, this man said. It had been a brush with disaster, and "Member Number 28" is relieved that the matter had ended the way it had: "I say praise be to Allah that we were arrested before we committed a crime or harmed the Muslims."

The faith assaulted and the faith confirmed: the retrieval of the ground lost to the extremists was not an easy enterprise. The upheaval ignited by Juhayman al-Utaybi in 1979 had come full circle. It had been deemed prudent to give theocratic puritanism an unfettered run, and bureaucratic institutions to support it, and considerable treasure. Now, moderation was the way out, and obedience to those in the religious and political hierarchies, and mercy to outsiders who uphold rival truths. The new official stand against extremism carried with it an admission that the obscurantists and the diehards had fed at the trough, and that the state had indulged them.

Deliverance—a good measure of it—came in the most unexpected of ways. The escalating violence that hit the country in the critical period of 2003–5 tipped the scales against the militants. Terrorism frightened the Saudi population. It had come in steady, spectacular episodes after the first attack of May 23, 2003. Car bombs struck a residential compound in Riyadh in November of that year to brutal results. In the year that followed, there were attacks again in Riyadh against the security forces and in the city of Yanbo against Western expatriates. Vaunted symbols of the state—the Ministry of Interior itself—were not spared. The oil complex in the Eastern Province came under attack as well. Al Qaeda was on the ground in Arabia and had bet it all on armed confrontation with the state. This was a battle the militants could not win. They were no match for the state; they had presented the population with a stark choice, and mainstream society opted for the comfort and the shelter of what it knew and lived with. The forces of order drew from the full spectrum of Saudi society. The society had drawn back as it watched ordinary policemen being cut down by the militants. The state and its organs played this with skill. There were the life histories of many of those who fell in the line of duty. If a struggle played out between the state and the militants for the sympathies of the broad population, the state won it outright. Those who had winked at the violence now ducked for cover. The fear of the unknown and the untried had worked to the advantage of the dynasty. The violent struggle took some thirty months to settle. By December 2005 the matter had been settled: Al Qaeda's Ayman Zawahiri conceded the fight in a message entitled "Impediments to Jihad." The Al Qaeda franchise in Saudi Arabia, he admitted, had been dealt a devastating blow.

There was more to the victory of the dominant order than the superior firepower of the state. Oil wealth, the purse of the state, was no small factor in tranquilizing the realm. A stock market frenzy had seized Arabia; the state would draw down its debts, and in one of those capricious shifts that men are given to, the passions would subside and cold calculations of interest would carry the day. Where the state had taken in $63 billion in oil revenues in 2002, those would rise to $162 billion in 2005, to $203 billion in 2006. (When the oil treasure was counted, the Saudi state had taken in something in the range of $1.1 trillion between 2003 and 2008.) Where the debt as percentage of gross domestic product was a staggering 120 percent in 1999, it would be drawn down to 27 percent in 2006, and to a paltry 5 percent in 2007. Infusions of wealth are of course double-edged: they can undo political orders or deliver them from troubles. This Saudi windfall was a great boon to the state. That innate sense of desert practicality and acquisitiveness prevailed. The Saudis had played a devastating role in the events of 9/11, and in the wars and the vigilance that followed. In one of those cruel ironies of history, they would sit on the sidelines as American power engaged in great taxing struggles in Afghanistan, Iraq, and beyond.

The Saudi state did an about-face on the American war in Iraq. The Saudi rulers had given the war a green light; in their fashion, they had waited for the Bush administration to make the final decision to go to war before they themselves committed to this endeavor. In the second of his four books on the history of the Bush presidency, *Plan of Attack* (2004), Bob Woodward tells that the long-time Saudi envoy to Washington, Prince Bandar bin Sultan, had been briefed about Washington's plans for the war four months before its onset. He had given his government's blessing but said that in return for Saudi help, the House of Saud expected their country to "play a major role in shaping the regime that will emerge not only in Iraq but in the region after the fall of Saddam Hussein." There was no love lost in Riyadh for the Iraqi despot; if Washington had finally decided, after more than a decade of paralysis, to be rid of him, the House of Saud was ready to ride with the Americans.

But this ride would have to be by Saudi terms: it was discreet and secretive, war had to be an option of last resort, and the door would be left open for Saddam Hussein to take his looted wealth, and his family, to a comfortable exile. In truth, the Saudis wanted a change of regime in Baghdad that would retain Sunni primacy. They did not possess the powers of prophecy; the kind of upheaval that would play out in Iraq was not foreseen by them, or by the war planners in Washington. The war would beget an Iraq altered beyond recognition. The Shi'a of Iraq, quiescent for a millennium, would rise from a long slumber. A community of lament and historical passivity rose to stake a claim to its country. Neither the Americans nor the Saudis had anticipated the rise of this new Iraq. The influence the Saudis sought in Iraq could not be had in a country in the grip of a bitter war. The Sunnis of Iraq refused to reconcile themselves to their loss of dominion; they ignited a war, a terrible season of slaughter, and they lost. Saudi Arabia could not reverse the outcome in Iraq; no Saudi (or Egyptian or Jordanian) cavalry was to ride to the rescue of the Sunnis.

The balance of power in the Persian Gulf had been altered, and room had to be made for a Shi'a-led government in Baghdad. This was a verdict the Saudis were unwilling to accept. They were to do some revisionism of their own. The war they had supported would now be branded a great strategic blunder. Fittingly, the same historical material reported by Bob Woodward confirms the change in the House of Saud's sense of this American project in Iraq. By the time of the events in Woodward's fourth volume, *The War Within* (2008), the old green light given the war was forgotten, and Abdullah, now monarch in his own right, had become a bitter foe of what the war had wrought. It is April 2006, a time of great difficulty in Iraq; an American diplomat, David Satterfield, is dispatched to Riyadh to meet with the Saudi ruler. The king has no patience for the briefing: the Americans, he says, had handed "Iraq to Iran on a golden platter. You have allowed the Persians, the Safavids, to take over Iraq." The Safavids, the dynasty that brought Shi'ism to Iran in the early years of the sixteenth century, were gone and forgotten, but this was the label flung in the face of the Iraqi Shi'ites by their Sunni detractors, and such was the dominant worldview in Saudi Arabia. "I warned you about this," says the king. "I warned the president, the vice president, but your ears were blocked. I have no interest in discussing this further."

The Saudis could protest that the "execution" of the war was not to their liking; they could, alongside so many others, maintain that the conduct of the war had shown enormous ineptitude. But their objections were rooted in the very Wahhabi creed itself. A sect of outsiders had arisen in Iraq; their culture reeked of rituals the Saudis loathed, indeed banned in their own country. Arabia was possessed of a healthy measure of xenophobia, an unease with difference. Iraq tested—and pushed at—that Wahhabi unease with "the other." In their outrage that this American war begot a radical new polity in Iraq, the Saudi rulers were at one with their public and with the religious scholars of the realm. It would be easy for them to rewrite the history of that war and to feign that they had nothing to do with this project of American folly. The skies over Iraq had been monitored from the Prince Sultan airbase, and it was from that base that the air campaign against Saddam Hussein had been launched. But the American forces and crews had withdrawn by August 2003. By then the costs of an open alliance with the Pax Americana had risen. This was quite early in the Iraq war, and the years would only sharpen the Saudi unease with America's work in Iraq. Colonel James Moschgat of the 363rd Air Expeditionary Wing had given the withdrawal of U.S. troops from the airbase a soldier's retrospect. "The mission thrived and prospered here, and I believe our legacy will live on. It's bittersweet, but it's time to go" (*New York Times*, September 22, 2003). The commander had been generous, but he was right to assert that an era had come to an end. If nothing else, the Saudis are consummate observers of power: the authority of the Bush administration was draining at home, opposition to the Iraq war had taken hold in Europe, and that fabled "Arab street" (read: the Sunni street) had declared this war nothing less than a colonial assault on an Arab land. It was the better part of wisdom to duck for cover and go with the crowd.

An Iranian bid for power was unfolding in the region, and the Saudis could not grant the Iraqi Shi'a the benefit of the doubt; they couldn't bring themselves to believe that this community of Shi'a Arabs could keep Iran at bay. The new political class in Iraq would give it a try. One of the shrewdest of Iraqi leaders, Shaykh Humam Hamoudi, a cleric-politician from the leadership of the Supreme Council and a parliamentarian with pedigree and education, narrated for me the details of a meeting he had with the head of Saudi intelligence, Prince Muqrin bin Abdulaziz (a half-brother of the king). Hamoudi sought to reassure his Saudi interlocutor that Iraq's leaders were keen on preserving their independence in the face of Iran's ambitions. He told Muqrin that a Shi'a-led government in Baghdad would make a better neighbor for Saudi Arabia than had been the case under Saddam Hussein. Saddam had been overbearing, it had been a nightmare for Saudi Arabia to keep him at arm's length. He had extorted money, he had invaded Kuwait, and he had tormented and bullied his neighbors in the Arabian Peninsula and the Gulf in the name of militant Arab nationalism. A Shi'a-led government, Hamoudi argued, would be content to live and let live, it would make the better neighbor if only because it would always understand its "differentness" from the Sunni Arab states around it. The argument was subtle, but it did not carry the day. By early 2008, other Arab governments at odds with the order in Iraq—the United Arab Emirates, Jordan, Egypt, even Syria's radical rulers—would signal in word or deed, by visits to Iraq, that they had accepted the new verdict in Baghdad. The Saudis stood apart, their suspicion of this new polity ran deep.

The rulers and the clerics did not have the play on Iraq all to themselves. There were the jihadists, predominantly young Saudis eager and willing to make their way to Iraq. A trove of documents and computers captured by the American military in a desert camp near Sinjar, by the border with Syria, in September 2007 laid bare the role of the Saudi jihadists in Iraq's mayhem. Out of 700 foreign fighters who crossed into Iraq in the preceding year, 305 were Saudis. (The Libyans ranked second, their distant country a veritable prison in need of repair;

charity should have begun at home, but it was easier to venture to Iraq in search of redemption and heroism.) The steady propaganda campaign against Iraq had put the neighboring country beyond the pale, and young militants could be forgiven the thought that "holy" war in Iraq was God's work.

The Saudi jihadists came in two distinct categories: *muqatils* (fighters) and *intiharis* (suicidals). This was a closer field of battle, geographically and linguistically, than Afghanistan, the culture nearly identical to their own. Wahhabi raiders had sacked Shi'a holy cities in Iraq in times past, and the new warriors could reenact the deeds of their righteous ancestors. A Saudi jihadist making his way to the safe houses of Anbar Province or Baghdad could be forgiven the thought that he was doing God's work in Iraq. All around him the media were saturated with nothing but enmity toward the Americans in Iraq and toward the *rafida* (the Shi'a heretics) coming into a new sense of power in Baghdad.

The biographical sketches of these fighters show younger Saudis drawn from mainstream society—former members of the National Guard, a *muezzin* (a man who calls the believers to prayer), a student of the Arabic language, a lawyer, a licensed electrician, a teacher, a physical trainer, a university student, a bank clerk, etc. Geographically, these fighters were representative as well: forty-five had come from Riyadh, thirty-eight from Mecca, twenty from Buraida and its surroundings, thirteen from Jeddah, twelve from Medina. There was wealth in the realm, and the Saudis came with respectable sums of money. Some had brought their own money, more had carried funds raised for them in local mosques. The Syrian "contractors" and middlemen who led the jihadists to the border with Iraq helped themselves to a good share of that money—no zeal for the Syrians, just an opportunity to fleece these gullible men traveling into deadly territory. A student from Mecca brought with him 5,190 Saudi riyals; the Syrians helped themselves to all of it. A lawyer from Riyadh brought with him 10,000 riyals; the middlemen kept half of it. A teacher from Riyadh brought with him a staggering sum, 22,300 euros. He handed "some money," he said, to the Syrians, exactly how much he did not say. Nadi Marzuq Khalaf of Riyadh, twenty-four years of age, brought with him 350 riyals and 10,000 Syrian liras. The Syrians took "everything by force," he said, "they demanded it." A fighter from Riyadh by the name of Khalid Muttaire brought with him a "pack and a half"—$1,500. His Syrian handlers took a pack and a half, they "asked me for it." The story repeats: the *muezzin* who brought with him 90,000 riyals said the Syrians took 80,000, and two mobile phones. These fighters came without mercy, but they were dupes as well: they hadn't been given a better, saner world. For the Syrians who escorted them to the border, it was all in the nature of a day's work. In the age of oil, the desert Arabs had become a source of livelihood for many "northern" Arabs. The jihadists were of a piece with that traffic.

The ways of the jihad, and of the jihadists, were illuminated for me in a chance encounter in Jeddah with two brothers of a young man I shall call Anwar Qahtani, who had made his way to Iraq and had been killed there. The brothers spoke of him with a subdued resignation. I had pressed for a narrative of their brother's life, and they obliged. Anwar, born in Saudi Arabia in Jeddah, was of Yemeni background—from Hadramout, at that,

Bin Laden's ancestral land. He was a workingman, he had followed his brothers into their trade. But he had been dissatisfied with his life, he had wanted more for himself. He had yearned for admission to the university, but had been denied. He had not been given Saudi citizenship. It was the luck of the draw; he had uncles who had been granted citizenship, and cousins who were given that privilege, but he was without citizenship. He had married a Yemeni woman but was unable to secure permission for her to join him. On the surface of things, he had reconciled himself to all that. He played cards in evening gatherings (indeed it was at the gathering of his old clique that the brothers were giving me the account of his life). He sang and was good at the drums called the tabla. His brothers insisted that there were no signs of trouble that they could see. But an American-educated scholar of high birth and an eye for his country's ways gave a different version. In the final months of his life in Jeddah, Anwar had grown depressed and less talkative. His beard grew longer, he gave up the *qutra* (the traditional headdress of the Saudis) for the headgear of Yemen. He told his brothers that he was leaving for a short visit to his wife and infant child in Yemen. But he confided to a friend that he was on his way to Iraq.

Anwar Qahtani hadn't stayed long in Yemen. He had gone to Iraq after a brief stopover in Syria. He was killed soon after his arrival in Iraq. The terrible news of his death was delivered to his family through the cell that had facilitated his passage to Syria. The jihad may be said to have its consolations, but the death of this man broke his mother and unhinged his wife. The family had grown concerned that the wife could take the life of her own child. The brothers had told of the life of a jihadist, but the American-educated social scientist who had arranged for this encounter had an interpretation of his own. His narrative was made of the disappointment in Anwar Qahtani's life— the opportunities he yearned for and was denied, the humble means. The regime, he said, and the Americans who take the regime's truth at face value, insist that it is all about belief and ideology, while it is in truth about the socioeconomic facts of the country, the modest means of those who prefer the jihad to the frustrations of normal life. My host was the same age as Osama bin Laden; they had gone to the same school and knew one another. He remembered him as shy and polite and "never a leader." But Osama, a child of privilege, was the exception; the norm were ordinary young men of limited means taking up the jihad because avenues of mobility are denied them. In the story of Anwar Qahtani he saw a man pressed by life and finding in the jihad in Iraq a religiously blessed form of suicide. It was easier, my host said, more flattering for the rulers and their truth, to attribute this phenomenon to psychological theories of unsettledness, to the gullibility of younger men who cast their chances aside in pursuit of a religious utopia.

"Go look at our young men, the pool from which the militants are drawn," he said. "They don't have decent medical care in a country rich with oil. They are unwanted in their own land. The best they could do is try to get hired as security guards at the entrance of the big hotels and the large business concerns. They're truly superfluous, they are proud, good people but they are trapped." A point was made for my benefit. At the end of a long day, he drove me to the Jeddah Intercontinental, and at the checkpoint we had to go through, he made sure to inquire about the young security guards. They were men both from Jeddah and from the countryside. This was the best they could do, this modest work at paltry pay. He told me of a nascent movement, "Saudi for Saudis," with its own website, made up of young people. They are "nativists," he conceded, they are disaffected from the rulers and the big merchants alike. They wish to reclaim their country, they want a share of the wealth and the spoils. "They will not succeed, the deck is stacked against them, there are more skilled and cheaper Filipinos and Indians to do the technical work, there are more pliable Egyptians. So these young people turn inward, or escape into religious solace."

The trail of these superfluous young men finding in the jihad religious merit and a substitute for the confinement of their life was illuminated by testimony given by a twenty-seven-year-old Saudi picked up in Iraq. He told his story in captivity, in the Green Zone in Baghdad. There was nothing unusual about the man, Muhammad Abdullah al-Obayd; his themes narrated in *Asharq Al-Awsat* (October 12, 2009) echo those told by Anwar Qahtani's brothers in Jeddah. The young man had been a history student before he made his way to Iraq. A fellow student at the Imam Mohammad Ibn Saud Islamic University in Riyadh had approached him about joining the fight against the Americans in Iraq. He had given him some literature about Al Qaeda and some DVDs. There was a band of militants at the university, and Muhammad al-Obayd joined them. He was told that he had a choice to make: he could join "the fighters" now or forget about the entire endeavor. Once the jihad called him, he never went back to the classroom and "never looked back." He told his family that he wanted to make the pilgrimage to Mecca; they gave him five thousand riyals (about $1,300) and wished him well. In early 2006, he took a bus to Bahrain, where a prepaid air ticket provided by the supporters of the jihad awaited him. He then traveled to Damascus through Dubai.

The contact in Damascus arranged for him a journey to Aleppo. There he joined a group of fighters drawn from Yemen and Tunisia and a number of other Arab lands. They were taken to the Syrian-Iraqi border and shown the road to the Iraqi town of Qaim. He was given a cell phone and a forged Iraqi identity card. He and his companions found their way to Anbar. For himself, Obayd chose to be a *muqatil* rather than an *intihari*. He wanted to learn the use of firearms and he wanted the experience of combat.

It so happened that Obayd joined the fight weeks before an American strike located and killed the Jordanian-born leader of Al Qaeda in Iraq, Abu Musab al-Zarqawi. "This was the time of the big battle with the Americans. I planted many roadside bombs, and I was one of three best marksmen in the group. I know I killed many people, how many I don't know. I am sure I killed American soldiers." His material needs were looked after by the insurgency, and he was given a monthly stipend of forty dollars. He lived with an Iraqi family, sharing the room of their sons, who were fighters as well. When he intimated that he favored one of his hosts' daughters, he was given her hand in marriage. The newlyweds agreed that no children would be born to them because "my wife wanted to be a martyr. There were many women at the time who yearned for martyrdom. Her parents supported her in that desire. We began to make plans for her martyrdom, and I was proud of her." "Martyrdom" apparently lost out, the wife turned up pregnant. For the first time in three years, Obayd called home; he and his wife wanted to leave for Saudi Arabia. "I told my family everything, I told them of my desire to go back to my homeland, and they said that they would arrange everything for me." Iraqi intelligence was on his trail, they had been listening in on the conversation. In early 2008, at a checkpoint on the road to Baghdad, he was picked up. He had no regrets, he had been happy to join the holy fight.

This young fighter gave the (Saudi) thing away. He had fought and he had killed, but he still wanted a way home, and an indulgent family and a country with means were still willing to have him back and to have him resume the normal life he had warred against in a neighboring land.

CHAPTER FOUR

A Rescuer's Line

The Iraq war and the jihad in nearby Anbar and Baghdad were on the margins of Saudi life. Four or five years after 9/11, after the (usual) speculations about the troubles of the Saudi state, the ship had been steadied. There was that Arabian luck which had seen this realm through many a crisis, and it would come in the nick of time. In the summer of 2005, the ailing King Fahd, incapacitated for the full length of a decade and barely conscious of his surroundings, died and was succeeded by his half-brother Abdullah. Fahd had taken the country through a great ideological fight with Iran in the 1980s and had seen it through Saddam Hussein's challenge in 1990–91. He had been shrewd but self-indulgent, and generous to a fault with his children and retainers. He had been something of a libertine in his earlier years; it took some imagination—and a generous suspension of disbelief—to label him Custodian of the Two Holy Mosques. His personal history had left him at a severe disadvantage in his dealings with the religious reactionaries.

Abdullah was Fahd's opposite: tight with money and with the treasure of the state, disciplined, and keen to repair the realm. True, he had had a long period as an understudy for Fahd, but kingship was to give him greater authority and self-confidence. He no doubt saw himself in the role that had been played to perfection by King Faisal, who had come to the rescue in 1964 when his older brother Saud had placed the realm in jeopardy with his extravagant ways and self-indulgence. Abdullah led a successful push to take his country into the World Trade Organization. The religious establishment had opposed that bid. The jurists had complained that membership in that organization would compel the country to trade in pork and liquor, and that the *sharia* would be trumped by foreign laws. The clerics were overridden; the economic reforms and transparency sought by Abdullah would be defended as needed concessions for membership in that world body. If a fight to keep the social and religious peace of the land was under way, Abdullah was the better standard-bearer. If the Saudi-American relationship required new terms of engagement, this new monarch would be the one to draw them. He wanted distance from the Americans, it was his way of displaying greater fidelity to Arab and Muslim loyalties. He was unsparing in his opposition to the Iraq War. He saw President George W. Bush's "freedom agenda," unfurled in 2003, as a threat to his dynasty and his country, an intervention at once dangerous and naïve in the internal affairs of the Arabs.

In a memorable formulation, Ibn Saud, who sought and obtained British patronage but made sure he was not hurt by Britain's embrace, spelled out his attitude toward his benefactors: "England is of Europe, and I am a friend of the *Ingliz*, their ally. But I will walk with them only as far as my religion and honor will permit." In the same vein, this son of the founder of the dynasty sought some distance from the Americans. He did so perhaps

secure in the knowledge that the American security guarantee
would still be there in a time of peril. Abdullah was too old, and
too wary, to wager on some new, untested doctrines of how international order is secured in our time. He courted the Chinese,
and hosted Russia's president on Saudi soil, but he had no illusions about the Chinese or the Russians or the Indians rushing to
the aid of his country in the face of a major threat. America was
fickle, the Saudis knew, they did not want to be too close to it lest
they burn, too far lest they freeze. They had successfully warded
off George W. Bush's "diplomacy of freedom," they had kept the
Americans out of their affairs; they had waited out that period of
American assertiveness (2001–6), and could experience a sense
of relief as the Bush administration sputtered to the finishing line.
Bush had "circled" the Saudis, and the Egyptians for that matter.
He had tried to prod them, push them in the direction of reform
and openness. It hadn't worked. The oil markets worked in favor
of the Saudis, and the Egyptian ruler had hidden behind his country's reflexive suspicion of foreign powers. In November 2007,
with little more than one year left of the Bush presidency, the
administration had convened a conference in Annapolis, Maryland, aimed at securing Israeli-Palestinian peace. It was too late
in the hour, but this was the kind of diplomacy the Saudis fully
mastered. They were unsentimental about Annapolis's chances
of success; they hadn't wanted the conference, but they showed
up for it. There was safety in numbers: nearly fifty countries and
international organizations were there as well. There was no point
in picking a fight with the Americans, no need to squander political capital on a symbolic occasion. The question of Palestine was
not about to be resolved, nor was it going to go away.

The Americans probe, and the Saudis hunker down: this has been Saudi Arabia's way with the Pax Americana for as long as America has had dealings with the Saudi state. In the war on terror, the Americans were keen to disrupt the money trail, to cut off the sources of terrorist financing. The Saudis promised cooperation, but that opaqueness of the realm and of its charities was a great barrier. Very little had come of that 2002 pledge to establish oversight of the charities. In February 2008, the leading American official who had been tracking terrorist financing, Treasury Department under secretary Stuart Levey, charged that millions of dollars were being raised in Saudi Arabia, and in the other oil states of the Gulf, and given to terrorist organizations. Levey was blunt when it came to Saudi Arabia's place in that money trail: "If I could somehow snap my fingers and cut off funding from one country for terrorism, it would be Saudi Arabia." The realm was big and inaccessible, nearby there were offshore banking centers in Dubai and Bahrain that could launder and conceal and transmit money. The Americans were destined to be locked into this cat-and-mouse game with the Saudis.

In November 2008, in one of those sudden seismic shifts in the American landscape that shall forever bewilder foreign observers, the American electorate chose for its political standard-bearer a newly minted U.S. senator, an African American, with a Muslim pedigree on his father's side. The Saudis had not known Barack Hussein Obama. In truth, they had kept their distance from this American election. Back in 2000, they had been heavily invested in the contest between George W. Bush and Vice President Albert Gore. They had sweated out that drawn-out drama. They hadn't thought much of Gore; in their eyes he was an unabashed supporter of Israel, he was heir to Bill Clinton, and they had never taken to him either. The dynastic element in George W. Bush's election greatly appealed to the Saudis; after all, this was George ibn George Bush, and the Saudi rulers had known and trusted Bush senior. In contrast, the contest between John McCain and Barack Obama elicited no great interest in Arabia. In his years in the Senate, McCain was not the sociable politician the Saudis favored. He was an American nationalist; on the stump, he had promised an energy policy that would secure American independence from "countries that don't like us very much." The Saudis knew they were the principal target of his remark. All along, he had been skeptical of the Saudi claims that they were serious about prosecuting the war on terror and cutting off the sources of terrorist financing. The American electorate would make this decision, and the Saudis would live with the new American president.

President Obama would send mixed early signals. He was done with George W. Bush's "diplomacy of freedom," he would pursue a foreign policy of realpolitik. For his first message to an Arab-Islamic audience, he had chosen a Saudi-owned forum based in Dubai, Al-Arabiya television. (This television channel had the advantage of being the un–Al Jazeera, as it were.) In that interview, he promised a return to the "respect and partnership that America had with the Muslim world as recently as twenty or thirty years ago." Obama was no revolutionary in foreign affairs, and the new tone was reassuring for Arab rulers unnerved by George W. Bush's Wilsonianism. There were, though, hints of Jimmy Carter in Obama—a belief in multilateralism, an olive branch to the Iranians, a willingness to reach an accommodation with the rulers in Damascus. This was a president carried into office by a massive financial crisis at home: he looked at burdens abroad with a jaundiced eye. He would not push the Saudis on matters of internal reform, nor did it seem likely that he would pursue a muscular foreign policy in the face of America's and Saudi Arabia's rivals in the region.

President Obama had come into office with a blueprint for "engaging" Iran. The Saudis could only wait—and puzzle over the direction of American policy in the Persian Gulf. They had made their own uneasy peace with Iran. They had watched the Bush administration's mix of rhetorical belligerence toward Iran and passivity in the face of Iran's growing claims of power. They had correctly concluded that there would be no strike against Iran, and no bargain with it during President Bush's tenure. Obama's promise of engagement—at least on the face of it—was more problematic. It awakened the dormant Saudi (and wider Arab) suspicion that an American deal with Iran would be made at their expense. It was hard to divine the mood in Washington as the new stewards of American diplomacy alternated between promises of engagement and threats of more biting sanctions. The president talked of accommodation, but his secretary of state held out the possibility of punitive sanctions and "crippling action" against Iran. The Saudis are no strangers to Washington's chaotic ways. The notion of a "defense umbrella" for the states of the region introduced by the secretary of state was as baffling to them as it was to the Israelis—perhaps as it was to the Americans pondering their options in Iran.

Three months into its tenure, the Obama administration dispatched one of its top Middle East hands, Dennis Ross, to

Saudi Arabia to lay out to King Abdullah the American policy toward Iran. Roger Cohen of the *New York Times* has supplied a telling narrative of this meeting.

> [Ross] talked to a skeptical monarch about the Obama administration's policy with Iran—and talked and talked. When the king finally got to speak, he began by telling Ross: "I am a man of action. Unlike you, I prefer not to talk a lot." Then he posed several pointed questions about U.S. policy toward Iran: What is your goal? What will you do if this does not work? What will you do if the Chinese and the Russians are not with you? How will you deal with Iran's nuclear program if there is not a united response? Ross, a little flustered, tried to explain that policy was still being fleshed out.

Is it any wonder the Saudis have survived so many obituaries of their doom? A few weeks after this briefing, chaos would engulf Iran in a very un-Saudi event: a presidential election. Crowds seized by both delirium and a sense of violation—with women in a prominent role, no less—would take to the streets. The upheaval came close to overwhelming the new Obama approach to the Iranian theocracy. From this sort of chaos, the Saudis averted their gaze. They no doubt derived some satisfaction from seeing the Iranian regime reeling at home. But a regime that abhors popular passions, and does all it can to keep its people out of the contests of politics, had no interest in seeing the Persian realm undone by popular fury.

There is a Saudi (perhaps a Najdi) pride in the indifference of the realm and of the people of the desert to the tumult, and the temptations, of the outside world. This prideful imperturbability was on display when President Obama came calling on the Saudi monarch in June 2009. Obama was on his way to Cairo for what was billed as his major speech, his outreach to the Islamic world. Cairo would celebrate him, but the Saudis barely took notice. I was in Saudi Arabia at the time; the earth did not shake, a young untested American leader had come to visit Arabia's wise and skilled monarch—the importance of the Saudi realm and of its monarch had been acknowledged. The media downplayed the visit. The Saudis, it was later learned, had not given the American visitor anything by way of diplomatic concessions. He was keen to restart the moribund Israeli-Arab negotiations and wanted help from the Saudis, and they had none to offer. They had a diplomatic initiative on the table, made back in 2002, and they would go no further. Egypt, Obama's next stop, would be more exuberant in its enthusiasm for the American visitor. Cairo was a city of fife and drums, but Arabia was not easily stirred, there was wealth there, and an ability to stand up to foreign pressures.

"The Saudis are second-guessers," former secretary of state George Shultz said to me in a recent discussion of Saudi affairs. He had known their ways well during his stewardship of American diplomacy (1982–89). This was so accurately on the mark. It was as sure as anything that the Saudis lamenting American passivity in the face of Iran would find fault were America to take on the Iranians. There is a congenital Saudi dread of big decisions. In a perfect world, powers beyond Saudi Arabia would not disturb the peace of the realm. The Americans would offer protection, but discreetly; they would not want Saudi Arabia to identify itself, out in the open, with major American initiatives in the Persian Gulf or on Arab-Israeli peace. The manner in which Saudi Arabia pushed for a military campaign against Saddam Hussein only to repudiate it when the war grew messy, and its consequences within Iraq unfolding in the way they did, is paradigmatic. This is second-guessing at its purest.

The Saudis have sway in the diplomacy of the region around them, but they are shrewd enough not to push their luck too far or to succumb to any illusions about their power. Yes, the Saudis were moved, perhaps offended, by the defeat of the Sunni Arabs in Iraq, which became so painfully evident in 2006–7. But their monarch never took the bait of posing as a savior of the Sunnis. It was one thing to tolerate bands of jihadists heading out to Damascus on their way to Iraq, quite another to take the plunge into the mayhem of Iraq. The Saudi ruler was under no illusions about the capabilities of Saudi forces or about the kind of power they could bring to bear on Iraq. He had watched the ordeal of America in Iraq, he knew that any Saudi intervention would be an act of great folly.

There is no love lost in the Saudi realm for the Persians or for the Shi'a Arabs. Where Saudi Arabia could contest Iran's push into Arab affairs without open, frontal warfare, the Saudis were willing to expend decent treasure and resources. But a big, costly duel with Iran was an altogether different matter. Lebanon is the test case of the Saudi way. The Saudi rulers care greatly about the political fate of Lebanon. (The more senior figures in the realm have a soft spot for that country; it had once been their playground, they had bonded with its notables and politicians and fallen for its guile and charm.) In a fundamental way, the Saudis are invested in the Sunnis of Lebanon; the erosion of their power relative to the Shi'a underclass weighs heavily on the Saudis. Demography, education, urbanization, young men of fighting age—and, yes, the coattails of Iran—had brought new, unprecedented power to the Shi'a in the 1980s and 1990s. The Saudis could not reverse the tide, but they waged a rear-guard action in defense of Sunni interests.

Political money matters greatly in Lebanon, and the Saudis underwrote the ride of an ambitious Sunni political contender, Rafiq Hariri, who had been born and reared in the coastal city of Sidon. Formed by the nationalism and pan-Arab outlook of the Sunni street that dominated Sidon in the 1950s and 1960s, Hariri had been born to modest circumstances. A bulldozer of a man, gifted and restless in the extreme, Hariri had made a fortune in Saudi Arabia in construction. He had risen through royal patronage; luck and drive had brought him to the attention of Crown Prince (later King) Fahd. Secure in his wealth, Hariri had itched for a return to the old country. He would reenter Lebanon with his own wealth and with Saudi political money. In no time, he was to overwhelm the Sunni merchant/ aristocracy of Beirut. They had been dismissive of him, he was an upstart, and, besides, he was not a Beiruti, and the Beirut Sunni bourgeoisie had a sense of its own primacy among the Sunnis of Lebanon. Hariri was to prevail, and the Saudi role in his ascendency was considerable. Until his assassination in 2005, Hariri's mission was the defense of Sunni rights and privileges in Lebanon. His politics were made in the Saudi mold: a dread of ideology, a defense of property, the shoring up of a Lebanese political order that would limit Iran's sway. He had been a skilled juggler, he had walked a fine, thin line between Saudi Arabia and Syria. The act had worked for nearly two decades. The shrewd

Syrian ruler Hafez al-Assad had played the game to perfection, allowed Hariri room for maneuver as part of Syria's broader relations with the House of Saud. But Hafez's heir, his son Bashar, lacked his father's touch and patience. Hariri was struck down to underline that a new man had come into his own in Damascus.

No sooner had Hariri been assassinated than the Saudis began to make no secret of their preference. They would throw their weight behind his son, Saad. Thirty-five years of age when his father was assassinated, Saad had been in no small measure a child of Saudi Arabia, he had lived a good many years there looking after his father's business interests. He had imbibed the rituals of Saudi court life—its long silences, its aversion to loners, its suspicion of crowds. (Saad had an older brother, Bahaa, but he was impulsive and flamboyant, more Lebanon than Saudi Arabia; he had been sidelined, and the Saudi royal court had played its role in giving the edge to the younger brother.) Saad Hariri was a good investment for the House of Saud. He would claim his father's fallen standard and in time assume the post of prime minister. He would balance the power of the Shi'a, and the Saudis would keep a discreet distance from the quarrels of Lebanon. On the face of it, the Saudis could insist that they harbored no animus against the Shi'a of Lebanon, they might even invite a Shi'a politician or two to Riyadh. There were rumors that they had bankrolled the campaign in 2009 of a young Shi'a politician at odds with Hezbollah. But no one was fooled, the Sunnis were the Saudi cause in Lebanon. A dynasty that held the Shi'a of the Eastern Province at bay was not about to travel to Lebanon in search of Shi'a allies. Saad Hariri was not at one with the princes of the Saudi realm, he would always be the son of a Lebanese courtier who made good in Arabia. But he could enter the Saudi world in a way denied his Shi'a and Christian compatriots.

The Saudis do not have the temperament or the desire for big ideological quests. They don't trust the region beyond their borders. The kind of fervor that played upon Cairo in the 1950s and 1960s, Baghdad in the 1980s, and the Iranian revolutionaries in the time of their zeal and enthusiasm is alien to the Arabian Peninsula. The Saudi means of "seduction" are rather limited; the strictures of Wahhabism, the separation of men and women, the aloofness and insularity of the Najdis set this realm apart. The sons of Ibn Saud have his guile, his recognition that the world beyond the Peninsula is full of menace and envy. The royals in Riyadh may savor the flattery offered by a northern Arab or two eager for Saudi patronage, but they have always seen through invitations that would take them out of the comfort, and safety, of their own world.

A "Sunni pact" of Arab states under Saudi leadership has a surface appeal to it, but the Saudis know better than to attempt it. Even in their very immediate neighborhood, in what should be their zone of comfort (the dynastic states of the Peninsula and the Gulf), the Saudi writ is rather limited. The smaller states march to their own beat. Qatar has an explicitly anti-Saudi thrust to its policies abroad and shows its fellow Wahhabi neighbor no deference. In the contest between Saudi Arabia and Iran, the Qataris have been more sympathetic to Iran's outlook. The freewheeling journalism of Al Jazeera has caused great discomfort in Riyadh over the years. The entire national ethos of Kuwait—its founding myth as a place on the Gulf to which tribes keen to escape the harsh limits of Central and Eastern Arabia migrated in times past, the walled city that resisted Wahhabi raiders—is at odds with the Saudi way. The parliamentary tradition of Kuwait is a big barrier between these two states, and Kuwaiti policy at home and abroad has always been strikingly independent.

Nor are matters any simpler between the House of Saud and the United Arab Emirates. There is an uneasy history of territorial disputes, and a determination by the rulers of Abu Dhabi and Dubai to carve out their own path in foreign and defense policies, and in the kind of liberties they will countenance. For all the talk of an anti-Iranian coalition in the Gulf, Dubai is an offshore base of the Iranian economy. Only the island state of Bahrain is willing to call the shots in accord with Saudi preference. This has to do with the economic dependence of Bahrain on Saudi Arabia, a dependence strikingly similar to Dubai's relationship to Iran. More important, Bahraini deference is a function of the sectarian dilemma of that island nation—a Sunni dynasty and security apparatus ruling a largely Shi'a population with historic ties to Iran. That causeway connecting Bahrain to Saudi Arabia is not only an economic pipeline for Bahrain and a safety valve for Saudis eager to escape the prohibitions of their country, but it is, as well, a protection of last resort for the Khalifa family that rules Bahrain. No one is under any illusions, rescue for the ruling Bahraini regime would come via the causeway from the Saudi realm should the need arise. Bahrain aside, the Saudis face prickly dynastic states sure that they can cut their own deals in the world.

For the House of Saud, above all there was no burning zeal in dealings with foreign entanglements. The Saudi rulers had come into an accommodation of their own with Hafez al-Assad in Damascus. The long peace held for three decades. The Saudi rulers were not enamored of al-Assad: he had taken plenty of their treasure; he had backed Iran in its war against Iraq in the 1980s; he had shown the Sunnis in his country no mercy. But he accepted the rules of the regional game, he gave the wealthy oil states cover in 1990–91 when Saddam Hussein made his bid for dominion. The Saudi-Syrian peace broke down after Hafez's death in 2000. His son slipped into Iran's orbit, he broke the code of protocol and decorum by dismissing his rivals in the Arab order of power as "dwarfs" and "half-men." And of course there was the assassination of Rafiq Hariri in 2005. He had thrown down a gauntlet to the Saudis in Lebanon, and in Palestinian affairs. He presided over a realm in economic disarray, but he still strutted around. He needed economic help and foreign investments in tourism and the service sector, and the Saudis responded with pressure of their own. They were Syria's largest foreign investors, they had injected some $900 million into the Syrian economy in 2006, and they let that figure slip to a paltry $15 million a year later. But as is their way, they did not give up entirely on the Syrian regime. By 2008–9, they were at work trying to "peel" Syria off from Iran, and to tempt Bashar al-Assad into cooperation. It was safe to assume that they loathed the inexperienced Syrian ruler, but he was at the helm in Damascus, and a new administration in Washington was courting him and holding out the promise of his rehabilitation. The Saudis would steal a march on Washington, they were eager to bury the hatchet with the man in Damascus.

In October 2009, less than five years after Hariri's assassination, King Abdullah made his first visit as monarch to Damascus. All may not have been forgiven, but it was time to move on and to heal the rift with the Syrian regime. There was a deal to be struck over Lebanon, divided between Syria's wards and Saudi Arabia's. Hezbollah was of course a case apart, a veritable Iranian instrument by the Mediterranean. Fidelity to Rafiq Hariri's memory and cause had run its course. There is an unsentimentalism to the Saudi way, and the Saudis had signaled to the devotees of Hariri who had turned his death into a cult of martyrdom that it was the better part of wisdom to let the matter rest. There is a Saudi way of dealing with death: burial in an unmarked grave, three days of mourning, and then a return to the normal world. This is the way of the desert, the farewell given king and commoner alike. The Hariri cult—his burial place turned into a shrine, the day of his death on February 14, 2005, marked as a time of mourning, the insistence of his followers that an international tribunal is sure to avenge him and to bring the killers and their accomplices to account—was destined to run afoul of Saudi "realism." And the Saudi monarch let it be known that since tens of thousands of Lebanese had perished in that country's war without end, there was something willful about worshipping at the altar of the fallen man.

No international tribunal looking into Hariri's murder was going to unseat the Syrian dictator, the Lebanese were no match for Damascus. Iran's threat had grown, and it was time to try to weaken the nexus between the Syrians and the Iranian theocrats. In the Saudi sense of things, the Arab order of power is best served by a workable trilateral arrangement of

Riyadh, Cairo, and Damascus. They would go the extra mile to accommodate Syria's rulers. The broad coalition of Lebanese Sunnis and Christians allied with Saudi Arabia—led by Hariri's son—had no choice but to accept the Saudi writ. Syria was nearby, a permanent menace, and her Lebanese critics were vulnerable targets for assassins' bullets and deadly car bombs. Furthermore, the specter of American power that had driven Syria out of Lebanon back in 2005 had receded. Lebanon was once again a marginal, small country of little consequence in the scheme of Pax Americana, and this Saudi-Syrian entente was a *fait accompli* that the Lebanese could not challenge. Lebanon was but a piece of a broader Saudi chessboard, and the Lebanese wards of Saudi Arabia were folded into a broader Saudi quest for defending their brand of order in their neighborhood.

Once the Saudis made their way back to Damascus, it was inevitable that their Lebanese protégé, Saad Hariri, now prime minister in his own right, would follow. In December 2009, he made his own difficult journey to Damascus, the matter of his father's murder was put aside as he called on Bashar al-Assad. There is an expression in the unsentimental world of the Levant of a man killing another, then walking in his victim's funeral procession. The Syrians had waited out the outrage and ostracism, the Hariri forces had insisted on Syria's culpability in the murder of their old leader, and now the son bowed to the inevitable. The two men, the Syrian ruler and his Lebanese visitor, it was reported, spent eight hours together, they talked of the past "without drowning in it," the sycophantic press reported. The Lebanese visitor, it was said, laid out to his host his view of Syria's old transgressions in Lebanon, while Bashar al-Assad spoke of the campaign of vilification that his country had endured the preceding five years. The Syrians were propriety itself. Hariri, though only a prime minister in the hierarchy of protocol, stayed overnight in a palace reserved for monarchs and heads of state. The men were in agreement, it was announced, on the positive role played by the Saudi monarch. There was no escaping the tyranny of geography and the inequality of power. Saudi Arabia was done with the Hariri assassination and with the campaign to isolate Syria in the Arab councils of power; its Lebanese wards were now ready to recognize the harsh facts of their weakness and vulnerability.

The "long war" on terror had shifted its central front from Iraq to the Afghan-Pakistani theater. No sooner had the Obama administration come into this inheritance than there was on display evidence that the U.S.-Saudi terms of engagement had not changed. The Saudis were there lending a helping hand in Pakistan, joining the United States in an effort to keep the Pakistani state afloat, offering an aid package of some $700 million at a gathering in Tokyo in April 2009. Pakistan mattered greatly to the Saudis as a hedge against Iran. A fortnight later, the American diplomat Richard Holbrooke, the special representative for Pakistan and Afghanistan, was on his way to Riyadh. The heart of his mission was the money trail yet again, that network of financing that led from a quiescent Arabian setting to Quetta and the Federally Administered Tribal Areas of Pakistan, on to Kabul and Kandahar. U.S. intelligence sources were confident that the Taliban drew on money generated from poppy cultivation and the opium trade, and from contributions that reached them from supporters in Saudi Arabia and the smaller Arab states of the Persian Gulf. Order at home, zeal and penchant for trouble abroad. There were Saudi financiers who could not countenance life under soldiers of virtue and terror, but they were ready to play with fire in lands beyond.

Saudis inhabit the modern world. Their world—the very piety they profess—has been made by their oil wealth and by the modern technologies bought by that wealth. Some years ago, in an astute set of observations, the Egyptian American scholar Mamoun Fandy, in his book *Saudi Arabia and the Politics of Dissent*, caught the complexity of Saudi society. He is worth quoting at some length:

> Saudi Arabia is a very complex mix of the "traditional," the various forms of modernities, and the postmodern, depending on the region and the sociocultural formation. For example, the Eastern Province is dominated by a Shi'a population, an oil industry, and an obvious U.S. presence. Highways, shopping malls, and expatriate communities give the impression of an American city, especially with the number of U.S. soldiers and civilians in Dhahran, Dammam, and Khobar. Except for the Saudi customs of closing shops for prayers and veiling women, these cities are a microcosm of global creolization. They contain at least as many foreign workers as Saudi citizens. Saudi children are raised by Asian and European nannies and are frequently bilingual. On the local level, hijabs and abayahs (local dress) are made in Taiwan and Hong Kong, and designer abayahs are made in Paris and London. Prayer rugs with a compass indicating the direction of Mecca are made in Japan. The holy places in Mecca and Medina are by definition part of global culture. Almost all religious icons sold outside

the Prophet's Mosque in Medina are made outside the country
and sold to foreigners as if they were Saudi-made.

There is an apocryphal Saudi tale about a Bedouin who had
spent a lifetime in the fierce desert and who, on a visit to his
relatives in the city, came into his first contact with the air con-
ditioner. "May paradise be the abode of he who came up with
this invention," the man said. His relatives were taken aback:
"But you have beseeched the Almighty on behalf of an infidel,"
they reminded him. "Give me a Muslim who would come up
with a similar invention and I will beseech Allah on his behalf
and on behalf of his parents," the simple *bedu* replied. The "infidels" are the source of much of the comfort of the Saudi world,
a modernist commentator observed in the pages of the most
enlightened of the Saudi dailies, *Al-Watan*, in late September
2009. "We can't pray for the undoing of the infidels while we
enjoy the fruits of their labor and inventions—all the way from
the airplane to the Internet to the soft drinks and the Viagra
pills. Here we are awaiting the formula for the shots against the
swine flu as some of us curse the West and hope for its undoing."

Wahhabism carried within it the risk of self-righteousness—
the risk, as David George Hogarth put it in his classic *The
Penetration of Arabia* (1904), of its adherents imagining that the
"eye of God is focused peculiarly on themselves." The Wahhabi
doctrine is a product of Najd and its culture. It is easy to write
for it a stark, solitary tale, an alternative history: a sect rises in
an unforgiving environment and then atrophies, or is undone
by mighty outsiders. Oil wealth and the modern state and all
the inventions of the dreaded infidels—the fax machine and the

internet, satellite television, the ease of travel—gave Wahhabism power and stridency. The struggle with Wahhabism, both within Arabia and beyond, is driven by a desire to see that creed come to terms with its own limits, to recognize the luck and the circumstances that enabled it to survive. In March 2009, the cinema made its appearance in Saudi Arabia. A Saudi comedy was screened twice a day for eight days in Jeddah. Tickets were sold, "we even sold popcorn," said the general manager of the studio which had made the film. More than twenty-five thousand people saw the film, women seated in the balcony, men in the stalls. The senior cleric who headed the Committee for the Promotion of Virtue and the Prevention of Vice declared the film an "evil" innovation. Several days later, he had a change of heart. Cinema was permissible, he said, so long as it was used "in matters that please Allah." Saudi society has been here before: change has stolen upon it repeatedly in the past, and the gatekeepers know when to let well enough alone.

The fight over the cinema was of no small significance to both its proponents and the militants. Weeks after its screening in Jeddah and Taif, that Saudi film came to Riyadh itself. This was Riyadh's first film showing in thirty-five years. The militants were prepared. After evening prayer, a dozen or so religious radicals turned up at the cultural center where the film was being shown to preach against the sins of the cinema. The police were there in full force as a buffer. Earthquakes and volcanic eruptions will happen because of the cinema, one diehard warned. Text messages were sent to the film's principal star asking God to bring about his ruin. The film was sparsely attended, security was tight, nine of the militants were arrested.

Those asserting the "normalcy" of the cinema and of movie houses were in truth attempting to retrieve past liberties. There had been no fewer than fifty movie houses in the country in days past, twenty-five in Jeddah alone. Sports clubs had had their own small movie theaters. Saudis flock to movie houses when abroad with their families. The ban on the cinema, the modernists argued, put the country on a par with Afghanistan under the Taliban, the only other Muslim country that enforced such a ban. This tribute to virtue was defective. Practically every Saudi home, even the poorest, had access to satellite television and the dish. In the privacy of their homes, thanks to satellite dishes that the most impoverished can afford, Saudis could sample the libertine fare of Italy, Germany, and Turkey. To their hearts' delight, they could savor the racy music clips of Lebanon (on Rotana, a channel owned by a member of the Saudi family, no less). It was hard manning the cause of virtue in an open world. The promoters of the cinema were sure that time and the desire of ordinary men and women were on their side. This confrontation would play out along a familiar divide between those who want to hustle Arabia into the modern world and those who don't. There had been battles within the royal clan itself over the introduction of television four decades earlier. There was a repeat of this now. The film at the heart of the controversy, a Saudi comedy, had been made by Rotana, an entertainment empire owned by Prince Waleed bin Talal. Amid the spirited debate about the film, it was revealed that Prince Waleed's brother, Khalid, had denounced the film and publicly broken with his brother over it. He had tried to advise his brother in private, he said, but Waleed would not mend his ways, and the making and marketing of this film was the straw that broke the camel's back.

"In Riyadh everything was forbidden, and everything permitted," a distinguished American-educated modernist, Turki al-Hamad, wrote in *Adama*, his coming-of-age autobiographical novel. Of his stand-in character, a Najdi young man who was raised in the Eastern Province and had arrived in Riyadh for university education in the late 1960s, Turki al-Hamad wrote: "Cinemas were nonexistent, but he watched the latest films there that were not even screened in Beirut or Cairo. Around any sports club or the film rental shops one could watch or hire any film one wished. . . . In Riyadh he saw overtly pornographic films." The risk of a public code as restrictive and severe as the Saudi code had become in the early 1980s is the risk of hypocrisy—that schizophrenia that separates what is said and avowed in Saudi public life and the way men and women live and make their way around unsustainable prohibitions. Arabs, Saudis included, may be particularly good at handling cognitive dissonance, but a heavy price is paid by societies that preach one code and live by another. This observation will have to stand: no society can be as good and wholesome and religiously observant as Arabia professes to be. The (real) life is whispered in private, and insinuated, and known for all its warts and imperfections, while the self-image is left intact and unchallenged.

The modernists are loath to admit it, but the prohibitions enforced by the *mutawwa*, and by the religious-bureaucratic institution that sustains them, are rooted in a wider conservatism, an unease with change. That peculiar institution, the Committee for the Promotion of Virtue and the Prevention of

Vice, weighs heavily on the society. Its intrusive enforcers are everywhere—in the shopping malls and on the road, on the lookout for "deviations" from public and religious decorum. Ironically, the Committee had been established in the 1920s when the puritans of the Najd and the Ikhwan conquered the worldly Hijazis. A buffer was needed between the two, a way of checking the scolds of the Najd. It was here where the system began, and it would, in time, spread to the entire realm. The Committee had acquired high official status, its leader was given ministerial rank, and there was money aplenty for it. Its enforcers were not the hardy breed of days past taking the rod to those who missed prayer, or flogging a poor soul caught smoking in public. The zealots now patrolled the streets in their GMC Suburbans, the treasure of the realm making possible, and lucrative, this peculiar enterprise.

The Office of the Inquisition in Castilian (and Spanish) history never had it so good. This Committee, it should be understood, cuts a big swath in the land. The most revealing statement about its power, and its reach, was made by the religious scholar who headed it in June 2008, Shaykh Ibrahim al-Ghaith, in an interview with *Asharq Al-Awsat*. This was a time when the Committee was under scrutiny, but its leader was unapologetic. There was a royal decree, the cleric said, dated September 7, 1980, which stipulated that "the state should protect Islam, apply the *sharia*, promote virtue and prevent vice." (Notice the date of the decree, less than a year after the seizure of the Grand Mosque and the turn of the state in favor of orthodoxy.) More powerful still, more binding than any ruler's writ, there was, the cleric reminded those who would question the legitimacy of his work, a "divine injunction," God's word in the Quran: "You are the best of peoples, evolved for mankind, enjoining what is right, forbidding what is wrong, and believing in Allah" (3:110). This was not a man to be intimidated by the laments of modernists worried about their worldly pursuits and their privacy.

A full sense of the resources of this institution is conveyed by Shaykh Ghaith's own startling statistics: In the course of the year 2006, the presidency of the Committee, he said, had conducted more than 47,500 "awareness and guidance programs" and distributed more than 7,830,000 pamphlets and audiocassettes. All this was in the domain of the Committee's first mission, the promotion of virtue. As for the second part, the prevention of vice, the cleric revealed that his operatives had dealt with 416,000 cases that involved 434,000 individuals—no less than 2 percent of the total population of the country—both citizens and noncitizen residents alike. The Committee had been merciful, he was keen to say. Some 392,000 individual cases had been resolved with discretion, only 42,000 individuals having been referred to the authorities. "No one is referred to the quarters concerned unless we see that such a referral is unavoidable."

No "reform" could contemplate the eradication of this institution, so integral had it become to the public order. The distinguished Princeton historian Michael Cook rightly observes that the "righteousness" within Saudi society was a substitute for the holy war on its frontiers. As the order of nation-states and territorial boundaries took hold, warfare against the infidels had come to an end. "If the Saudi state was not to lose its religious identity, it had to turn its righteousness inwards. . . . In effect, forbidding wrong within Wahhabi society had taken the place of holy war on its frontiers." There was no thought of dismantling this religious-bureaucratic apparatus. At best, this institution might be tamed and "softened," its abuses kept in check. In early 2009, King Abdullah had shuffled the deck and removed the Committee's leading cleric, signaling that he wanted to rein in the Committee and to regulate its affairs. The monarch had come down the middle in the debate about the Committee. "No to its cancellation, yes to its reform" was the new official mantra. A new religious functionary, a man in his mid-forties, a good generation younger than his predecessor, was to be the new leader.

The stakes in this struggle between the Committee and its critics were crystallized in a remarkable open letter to the new head of the Committee by one of the erstwhile religious firebrands, Ayid al-Qarni himself. Qarni's platform was a column in the influential daily *Asharq Al-Awsat* on March 10, 2009. Qarni welcomed the new man at the helm, "His Highness Shaykh Abdulaziz al-Humayyin," opening with a reminder that the appointment was part of the "renovation and reform" undertaken by the monarch. The modernists couldn't have had a better ally than Qarni, for he cut to the heart of what troubled them. "In Islam, we have no courts of inquisition that rejoice when a sinner is caught, and are eager to see the disobedient arrested; instead we have institutions of mercy, penitence administration, and councils for reconciliation and forgiveness. We are commanded by God to be discreet and to overlook errors if they do not constitute a threat to society, if they are not destructive, if they do not disturb the peace." The enforcers of the Committee had played havoc with the privacy of their suspects, and Qarni minced no words in this regard: "In Islam, spying and violation of privacy to get to know secrets are not permitted; instead there is guidance, with flexibility and gentle rendering of advice."

Qarni spoke to this senior cleric from within the tradition itself.

> Our Prophet, God's prayers and blessings be upon him, said: "He who knows discretion toward the weakness of a Muslim in this life, will be protected by God in this life and in the afterlife." A man came to the Prophet and told him he had caught a sinner, The Prophet said: "It would have been better for you to be discreet about what he has done." The Prophet used to protect those who erred; he would not name them, expose them, or injure their feelings.

Qarni had the perfect pitch. He was sure, he observed, that "His Highness the Shaykh" is likely to follow the Prophet's example and discretion. The proper advice is best rendered in private; that which is given in public is a "sort of reprimand" and nothing else. The bureaucratic apparatus of the zealots was put on notice. Larger numbers of Saudis were clamoring for the saving graces—and compromises—of normal life.

The long-running debate about the Committee and its work was joined—and clarified—when the Committee proposed installing surveillance cameras in the shopping malls and other public places. This was odd, the critics of the Committee and its methods protested. The zealots had always taken a severe view of photography, they had defaced magazine covers, they had a ritual of cutting out of magazines provocative pictures of movie stars and unveiled women, yet here they were advocating an intrusive new technology. The zealots were hoist on their own petard: to uphold "virtue" they had to gain access to the privacy of families, to intrude on the secluded domain of women. It was a sure thing that the installation of surveillance cameras would never get off the ground.

The enforcers of virtue were on the defensive. On June 1, 2009, in the Saudi edition of the pan-Arab daily *Al-Hayat*, there was a picture of a man of the *mutawwa*, surrounded by cameramen and a handful of spectators, bowling in an alley in a Riyadh shopping mall. He had his unkempt beard, the signature headdress without a cord (the *mutawwa* way). The thing looked scripted, he had been authorized to do it. A former student of mine savored the picture. The diehards will bend, he said, if the powers that be side with the modernist camp. The *mutawwa* were clearly on notice, they now had to work with the police and with the provincial governments, they needed arrest warrants where they had once been free to act on their own. They could not "out" their prey, defame them in public, or tell of their misdeeds. A man of the *mutawwa* in a bowling alley was not enough. The Committee centers were a law unto themselves. In Riyadh, there were more such centers than police stations. A watchdog institution, the National Society for Human Rights, wrote in 2009 about five losses of life at the hands of the *mutawwa* in Riyadh, Tabuk, Medina, and Najran. In guarded language, this watchdog organization noted the attempt of the Committee to deny or belittle these incidents or to write them off as individual acts. "It's compellingly important to determine the work mechanisms of the Committee staff, especially field workers among them, in such a way that people's liberties are safeguarded and at the same time the Committee staff members are enabled to perform their duties toward the community," the National Society for Human Rights observed.

The liberals may despair of it, but "commanding right and forbidding wrong" was demanding, steady work. Amid this debate, in Kharj, southeast of Riyadh, it was announced that the *mutawwa* had broken up a prostitution ring. A tip came to them about a Syrian woman active in the trade who had arranged for a "private evening" in a luxurious guesthouse for six of her girls and five men. In yet another item, at about the same time, the men of the Committee had arrested two well-known soccer players. They had been picked up in a Riyadh hotel in the company of two young women. Their mobile telephones had led to rounding up of other women. It was not the practice of the Committee, its spokesman said, to target particular individuals or entrap them. It was no fault of the Committee, he insisted, that the names of the soccer players had leaked. The *mutawwa* did their work without fear or favor, he added, they have always tried to protect the privacy of people brought up before the judicial authorities. The Committee's bureaucratic apparatus was precise about the merciful ways of its work. Less than 10 percent of the violations they uncover are referred to the judicial authorities. The rest are resolved on the promise that the violators would mend their ways.

The royals were skilled traffic cops: they held back the religious enforcers when their excesses grew particularly burdensome or notorious. But they gave into them as well. In July 2009, a dispatch from Jeddah carried news of a victory for the religious zealots. The minister of interior had issued a decree granting the *mutawwa* permission to "enter all seaside chalets in Jeddah, to monitor them daily so as to limit any unsuitable behavior occurring inside." The little liberties were always under siege. A month earlier, I had been at the seaside in Jeddah. I had gone to the beach house of a noted man of business and former official of the state. In truth, he was a royal, but a relative had instructed me to address him by his first name. The house was discreetly concealed behind a nondescript gate. The walls did not give away a place of luxury. Once within the gate, the drive led to a house in exquisite taste—immaculate landscaping, a dock at the end of a long walkway, the owner's yacht within sight. A big, gaudy house next door, out of place by the sea—it belonged to a royal, and my host looked upon it with despair and resignation—was under construction.

Saudi restrictions were a world away. My host held the political affairs of his country with the same resigned indifference that he reserved for his neighbor's architectural travesty. All political doors had been open to him, but the political game had not held him, he had retreated into commerce and into the saving graces of private life. He had retrieved from a quarry nearby two blocks of black marble that dated back centuries. He was proud of his find, he had them displayed in a corner of his garden, he savored their beauty as he was showing me the mango trees and the tropical vegetation he tended to. There wasn't much to say about politics in this land, he said in passing, he was of the royals, and he knew them as they were. He would not dwell on them, but he said enough to tell me that he didn't see much difference among the sons of Ibn Saud. Nothing would tempt him back into the political arena, he said. He had been close to the Crown Prince, but that was years back. He had the means and the standing for a private life, and for him this would do.

On the way back to town, I stopped by a marina—it was by the road, a gated community manned by private security. There was no *abaya* to be seen on the premises. It was night-time, but women and children were everywhere, there were boats and small yachts and countless Jet Skis. The marina could have been anywhere in the world, there was nothing that gave away its oddness against the background of Saudi reality. A few miles away, on the Jeddah boardwalk, it was a different world. Ordinary Saudis escaping the summer heat rolled out their mats, or simply sat down by their cars on folding chairs they had brought with them. There were groups of men spending the evening together, and there were families with children nearby. I couldn't help thinking of the fate of the young girls, and of the reprieve given them by childhood. Soon these young girls, now relatively free and unencumbered, would be pushed by puberty into the restricted space of women. Of this brief respite, they would have but a vague memory. The place was hard on its people, and watchful. The minister of interior cracking down on the private chalets could be forgiven the thought that Saudis beyond these private enclosures of the affluent are doubtless on his side. "The unsuitable behavior perhaps is women swimming," a commentary on this Jeddah dispatch added. The balance between piety and liberty had not yet been found.

The Committee for the Promotion of Virtue had mastered the game of press releases and public persuasion. It had going for it some of the deeply held phobias and predilections in the land. Its dispatches (I work here with a sample from June–July 2009) told of its enforcers cracking down on sorcery; indeed a "modern" unit, it was announced in late June, had been established to combat sorcery and to prevent those who dabble in sorcery and witchcraft from entrapping women in distress. And there was the steady flow of victories: the busting up of yet another prostitution ring, the arrest of a drug dealer who practiced his trade in proximity to a school for boys. An Asian gang had been undone—one woman and six men—its members had been caught making and selling moonshine; a Sudanese doorman had been using his workplace for purposes of prostitution and the Committee had caught up with him. Above all, there were these endless reports about witchcraft, and they kept the Committee men in the field with plenty to do.

In the minister of interior, the Committee had a powerful friend at court. In the royal sweepstakes occasioned by the serious illness of Crown Prince Sultan, the Committee's "vote" belonged to the minister of interior. Prince Naif had intervened in the matter of a film festival that had been in the works for the summer of 2009. He had banned it, and the pamphleteers of the Committee were fulsome in their praise of him. In the daily *Al Riyadh* (June 27, 2009), one of the Committee's leaders paid tribute to Prince Naif as "the first man of national security." This man's entire life, the writer said, had been dedicated to protecting the *sharia* and to affirming the "Islamic mission" of the Saudi state. "Prince Naif has never broken faith with the mission of enjoining the good and forbidding evil. He has always stood with our work, believed it to be our domain, in the same manner that medicine is left to physicians, engineering to engineers, and so forth."

The writer of this tribute gave the matter away. The Committee was fighting for its turf, its access to public treasure, its place in the public order. This senior prince, third in the line of hierarchy, was the Committee's protector and ally. The reformers could draw strength from the monarch, the enforcers of virtue from his half-brother. An American-educated bureaucrat from King Abdullah's entourage presided over the National Society for Human Rights, a government-constituted "liberal" watchdog. But on its side, the Committee for the Promotion of Virtue had a dedicated religious apparatus and the support of a contender for the throne. A cynic could write it all off as a "division of roles" among the brothers in the House of Saud—the reforming king, his half-brother the strict autocrat at Interior. It is a big royal clan, and there are princes for all kinds of seasons and casting calls. No outsider fully knew the play among the brothers. Those who talk don't know, those who know don't talk, said a shrewd businessman at the end of a long discussion about the ways of the royals. All hopes are invested in them— the religious reactionaries' determination to keep the orthodoxy intact and supreme, the liberals' expectations that the old ways could yet crack and be challenged.

The religious establishment often bends with the wind— in truth, it yields to royal prerogative when it has to, when the will of *wali al-amr*, the custodian of power, is at stake. This introduces a good deal of uncertainty and skepticism about the writ of the jurists. Things forbidden and *haram* are suddenly given a waiver, the gates that had been bolted are thrown wide open. Even the fierce gatekeepers of the Committee for the Promotion of Virtue and the Prevention of

Vice are given to this kind of sudden change, and the lay-
men are skeptical and knowing enough to understand that
orders had come from on high—from the monarch, or from
the all-powerful minister of interior—that brought about sudden shifts of opinion. In December 2009, the leading cleric
in the Province of Mecca, one Shaykh Ahmad al-Ghamdi, put
forth an opinion that the mixing of men and women, *al-ikhtilat*,
was in the nature of things organic to the lives of nations, and
those who hitherto had banned it hadn't really given the matter the attention it deserved. That thin, artificial line between
permissible and impermissible things in the country was
given a stark illustration.

A young Riyadh lawyer, known for his modernist, fear-
less positions, Abdul Rahman al-Lahem—the American Bar
Association gave him the International Human Rights Lawyer
Award in 2008—saw in this change in the position of so prominent a figure in the ranks of the religious enforcers yet further
evidence of the difficulty of an ordered life under the law. "It
doesn't concern me," the lawyer wrote, "if a shaykh awakens
from a long slumber, what matters is the logic that reduces the
law to the whim of a religious judge and to what goes on in the
mind of a shaykh." Abdul Rahman al-Lahem allows himself one
of the satirical notes that have landed him in trouble, on more
than one occasion, with the religious establishment:

> It has become a daily requirement, in the morning, for all in
> the Kingdom of Saudi Arabia, before heading out to work, to
> check the daily list prepared by our brothers in the Commit-
> tee for the Promotion of Virtue and the Prevention of Vice,
> for such a blacklist, of what is permitted and what is not, is

subject to daily change. That which was a vice in the night can become, with Allah's blessing, a virtue in the morning. In the end, the opinion of Ghamdi isn't of great interest to people, what matters is the quest for a legal order that specifies crimes and their punishment in a manner akin to other nation-states. Law should be the shaykh in our midst.

The irreverence of this young lawyer is the price the custodians of religion—armed with the writ and the sanction and the resources of the state—pay for their heavy-handed ways. The legal orders that stick on the ground, that have the consent of those whose lives are anchored in those orders, always run in tandem with prevailing practice and custom and tradition. The Committee and its zealots are no exception to this rule. A strict constructionism—to borrow a term from American legal practice—would need the wisdom to be silent at critical junctures on matters of great controversy, the subtlety in the face of truly contested issues of public life.

The pervasive question of women's subjection haunts the realm, but no resolution appears in sight. It often seems that the entire theology and cultural life of the land is reduced to the felt need to control the border between men and women, and to keep the women in the confines they have been relegated to. The watchfulness of Saudi society, the absence of joy in the public space, the dreariness of its media—they are all the inevitable outcome of a religious and moral code that segregates the sexes and places draconian limits on the lives of women.

John Stuart Mill never of course ventured into Arabia, or thought about the dilemma of its women. But a reading of his memorable treatise "The Subjection of Women" (1869) speaks to the damage that befalls cultures that accept, and codify, the inequality of the sexes. "The object of this essay," Mill wrote:

> is to explain as clearly as I am able, the grounds of an opinion which I have held from the very earliest period when I had formed any opinion at all on social and political matters: that the principle which regulates the existing social realities between the two sexes—the legal subordination of one sex to the other—is wrong in itself, and now one of the chief hindrances to human improvement; and that it ought to be replaced by a principle of perfect equality, admitting no power or privilege on the one side, nor disability on the other.

Mill was addressing the disabilities of women in Victorian England. Those pale in comparison with the restrictions placed on Saudi women. There was nothing in Victorian society that came close to the Saudi law of *Mahram*, which stipulates the guardianship of a male (a husband, a father, a brother) over the conduct of women—their right to travel, to have a passport, to open a bank account, in short, the right to all these things taken for granted in other lands. Saudi women suffocated by the restrictions placed on them are often given to reminding all who care to listen that these restrictions are not timeless, that they have been imposed in recent decades, that they are a byproduct of the oil wealth. (Kuwaiti liberals recall a time before oil when Kuwait City had a brothel in the middle of the city and alcohol was openly available.) Only a society exempt from the brutal laws of economic need and economic rationality could afford the ban on women driving, the broader restrictions on the freedom of women to move about, and the machinery of bureaucratic and legal control that keeps these discriminatory practices in place. Wajeha al-Huwaider, an outspoken, American-educated woman (she had made her way, alongside her husband, to Indiana and Washington, D.C.), a Shi'a from the Eastern Province, recently made that ironic, painful point. "It is interesting," she told the Kuwaiti daily *Awan*, in an interview published in July 2009, "that the mothers and grandmothers of today's Saudi women had all these rights, and enjoyed much greater freedom than today's women—as did all Muslim women in past eras, such as the wives of the Prophet. None of those women were subjected to this oppressive *Mahram* law, which is not based on the tenets of Islam and in fact has nothing to do with Islam."

Wajeha al-Huwaider's testimony is not unique. Echoes of it can be heard in the laments of so many Saudis concerned about the new power of the religious reactionaries. A man from the southwestern Province of Asir recalled the change in his own lifetime in his mother's behavior. She had once mixed freely with neighbors, shook hands with male visitors, joined in their conversation. Then it was as though a curtain fell on a whole epoch: she had grown religious, she would no longer receive even a young boy from the neighborhood. More startling to this man, his mother had accepted the change, she and so many others in this once-uninhibited part of the country came to view the past as a time of depravity, a time of *jahiliyya*, pre-Islamic ignorance. Men and women in Asir, this man added, once lived as though they were on stage: they cherished music and the song, they were away from Najd and its culture and its enforcers. Indeed, they prided themselves on their defiance of Najd, on their deep differences with that severe heartland. They knew that they were not trusted by the political-religious order based in Najd, that their loyalties were suspect and their ways held in contempt. But the dominant order prevailed, he concedes. It has all but extirpated the old ways of Asir. Nowadays, the locals drawn into the *mutawwa* are more severe than the Najdis, keen to demonstrate their zeal and sternness. The political-religious apparatus had been skilled; it had co-opted the tribes. "What was spared by the tribes, was cut down by the Wahhabi sword, what was spared by the Wahhabis was done in by the tribes." This man's mother, and younger people after her, made their adjustment to things beyond their power.

A remarkably similar account is rendered in a work of historical fiction—again, the fiction is mere disguise, a bow to necessity—by the political writer Turki al-Hamad in *Ri'h al-Jannah* (*The Wind of Paradise*), published in London in 2005. In this book, Turki al-Hamad picks up the trail of the death pilots and the Saudi "muscle" who were aboard the planes of 9/11. There is the needed narrative license in this book, but it is in the main a work of journalistic reconstruction of that time and of that band of jihadists. Two young brothers, Wael and Waleed, in Turki al-Hamad's book are easy stand-ins for Wael and Waleed al-Shahri, who were aboard American Airlines Flight 11, which crashed into the North Tower—this was the Mohamed Atta team. The two brothers were in the first-class cabin, side by side, seats 2A and 2B.

Turki al-Hamad is nothing but a man of the Saudi world, there are excursions into Hamburg and Cairo, but it is the Saudi background and the Saudi young men that interest him the most. The Wael and Waleed in his account are ordinary boys from the mountainous countryside of Asir. They love the fields beyond their village, but they dread the field work. They have a pious father, they have for him the respect—and fear—owed him in this culture. It is the father who hustles them to prayer at dawn. There is hushed talk in the family of a time when their father was less of a scold, but they themselves have no memory of that time. They have an older brother who quit the village for the lights of Jeddah and the security of a government job. The older brother comes home now and then, but he has no kind words for the stern ways of the household. One of the two future jihadists has a vague recollection of the girls bringing food to their fathers in the mountains, and he recalls as well the songs of an uncle who sang as he did his work in the fields. But that was before the village "found its way to the path of God."

That older time of indolence became a dreaded past that no one wants to remember. The mother of the future hijackers tells of that time when women worked the fields unveiled, when they went to hawk things in the market, and took part in mixed gatherings of men and women. "But praise be to God, the preachers, the *duaat*, descended on the province, they began teaching people the proper way, and women ceased receiving guests or working the fields or turning up in the markets. They donned the veil, we were living in darkness, but God the merciful delivered us into light. Had it not been for these *duaat* we would have been consigned to the flames of hell." All this happened, the storyteller says to her son, after the big event, the seizure of the Grand Mosque in Mecca in 1979. Once again, that event is seen as the divide between a time of an older freedom in the hill country and the discipline and unforgiving rigor of the new ways. Turki al-Hamad himself is a man from the town of Buraida in Qasim, with its pride of place in the strict Wahhabi orthodoxy. In his narrative, Qasim rides roughshod, and has its way, with the other provinces. These older traditions—and the liberties that came with them—are trampled upon.

That the damage to women is so pervasive need not be belabored. But young men denied normal access to the company, and to the world, of women are damaged as well. That odd brew of belligerent piety and sexual prurience and watchfulness that runs the society is the predictable response to the repression. We don't have the details and confessions and life histories of Saudi jihadists who cast caution aside to take up the struggle against the order at home (or in lands beyond) in order to draw that obvious connection between sexual repression and compensatory militant zeal. But from Afghanistan and Algeria to Egypt and the Arabian Peninsula, the "boys of the jihad" carry with them the burden, and the pain, of that separation from women and enforced abstinence. Mohamed Atta's last will and testament, found in a travel bag that missed its connecting flight on 9/11, spoke of a sexual disturbance and a misogyny surely not his alone. "Neither pregnant women nor unclean persons shall be allowed to take leave of me—I reject it," the young Egyptian wanted it known. "No woman shall beg pardon for me after my death. . . . Women shall not be admitted to my burial nor later find themselves at my grave." To desire and despise women at the same time, to attribute to them hidden, wicked powers that must be controlled: this is the fate of cultures and subcultures that keep the sexes apart.

To make his point about the connection between the freedom of women and "human improvement," Mill had written
that if his society persisted in denying women's rightful claim
to equality, "all that has been done in the modern world to relax
the chain on the minds of women" will have been a mistake.
"They never should have been allowed to receive a literary education. Women who read, much more women who write, are,
in the existing constitution of things, a contradiction and a dis-
turbing element; and it was wrong to bring women up with any
acquirements but those of an odalisque, or a domestic servant."
The Saudi realm has done much better, and gone much further,
than enabling women to read and write; it has enabled them
to attain the highest academic distinctions. Yet it continues to
hem them in, to deny them (and itself) the dividends of what
ought to be ordinary, unencumbered liberties. The rulers plead
that the prohibitions in the land are not theirs to overturn, that
these are matters of custom, and of faith, that they will atrophy
on their own, or they will be reversed by the religious scholars
whose domain they are.

As matters stand, women constitute 50 percent of the native
population of Saudi Arabia, but only 10 percent of the work-
force. In words that (unintentionally) echo Mill's about the
subjection of women, an enlightened commentator, Mshari
Thaydi, who had made his own journey into the world of the
religious diehards only to break with them, wrote of the contradiction between educating women and then denying them
the opportunity to work. "We cannot deny the fact that female
university graduates need work and a source of income, not to
mention their need to gain the moral satisfaction that comes

with employment. Otherwise, there would be no point in arduous study, attending university and paying university fees if it would lead only to women staying at home or fighting over jobs designated for women. Why then give them an education in the first place?" (*Asharq Al-Awsat*, October 24, 2009).

"My life has not changed much, for all the talk of reform," a proud younger woman in Jeddah, with the best of education, said with a mix of resignation and bitterness. She was a woman of considerable means, her husband a successful businessman. "I have five cars and two drivers, and I have to try to arrange my life in such a humiliating way so that I can have my children picked up from school. When I go to government ministries for official business, a notarized statement now and then, the normal business in a society burdened by all sorts of regulations, I am dismissed and told to return with my *Mahram*, my male guardian. The waste of it, things will never change, King Abdullah means well, but the old habits and the old ways have taken hold."

An older woman, a worldly widow who has known wealth and foreign travel, and years of exposure to Britain and the United States, spoke of the humiliation that came into her life after the death of her husband. Her son, she was told, was now her *Mahram*. She had raised and nurtured him, she had seen him get the finest American education; she bristled at the thought that she would need his permission to travel abroad, to conduct official transactions with the government bureaucracies. She had submitted to the old ways when her husband was alive, he had been indulgent of her headstrong ways, he had sheltered her from the slights. Now the boy she raised was entrusted with guardianship over her. We were in her splendid beach house on the Red Sea, an open lagoon lay before us, it was nighttime, and a lit-up walkway led to a pagoda over the water. She had secured the property, and the house reflected her taste; servants moved discreetly in the background, and the dinner laid out for us was again reflective of her style and worldliness. She spoke of her time in America, in the 1960s, with her husband, a young couple who knew America in those days when the color barrier between black and white divided American society. She marveled at the election of Barack Obama, knew the details of his electoral triumph. She and a dozen like-minded women, she told me, had laid out to then Crown Prince Abdullah their concerns over the disenabling limits on their lives. This was six or seven years earlier, the meeting had been arranged by Abdullah's wife. He promised he would do what he could, she had a soft spot for the man, but she, too, could not see him turning back the tide of religious reaction.

In late 2009, the fault line between the modernists and the religious reactionaries and the all-important question of women's place in the life and labor of the land came into sharp focus when the monarch inaugurated a much-trumpeted project that bore his name, the King Abdullah University of Science and Technology. This was a vision of Arabia's future, a state-of-the-art institution of higher learning with the most advanced technology, located on a desert plot on the Red Sea coast, some fifty miles north of Jeddah. Its curriculum was entirely technical and scientific, there would be no place in it for disputations of politics and the social sciences and the humanities. The king had nursed this project for nearly a quarter-century, the king's men said. He had granted the institution a $10 billion endowment; the bill for building the campus may have been in excess of $2 billion. Scientists and administrators from the world's preeminent institutions of higher learning were aggressively courted to staff and lead this institution. But the old matter of the mixing of the sexes was to rear its head. This university was to be a case apart, it was to be a coeducational institution. The upholders of the orthodoxy braved the storm. A member in good standing of the Council of Higher Ulama, one Nasser al-Shethri—an advisor to the royal court, at that—in an appearance on a satellite television channel that serves as a platform for the religious diehards opined that the "mixing of sexes is a great sin and a great evil." The cleric had crossed a red line; he was immediately stripped of his membership in the highest clerical body. The king spoke in no uncertain terms, he warned of extremists who "know only the language of hate, fear dialogue, and only seek destruction." The balance between monarch and cleric was laid bare: the cleric was chastened, he had been misunderstood, he had spoken out of love and regard for the Custodian of the Two Holy Mosques.

This was in keeping with an old tradition: the struggle over women's education had always been a seesaw affair. The state would probe what the society could bear; it would step back and let matters run their course, then it would throw its weight behind a tolerable consensus. This had begun in the late 1950s, and the Najdi heartland was particularly zealous in its opposition to the schooling of girls. Educators sent to Najd to open schools for girls were often set upon by the mob and had to seek sanctuary in government offices. We have an authoritative account of this struggle supplied by a Saudi scholar, Abdullah al-Washmi. There is vibrancy in the story he tells, in a book published in 2009 by a publishing house based in Morocco. (The life of culture is so curtailed in Arabia that a book of this kind must find an outlet in Casablanca, Beirut, or Cairo.) It is 1960, and a fairly tolerant monarch, Saud, and his crown prince, Faisal, are keen to introduce public education for girls. The Najdi city of Buraida opposes this "heresy." There is agitation in the mosques, money is collected to send a delegation to Riyadh to protest this unwanted innovation. Some eight hundred people make their way to Riyadh, led by a local judge. There, they encounter a stern Prince Faisal who is a believer in the cause of women's education. Schooling for girls is not compulsory, they are told; those who want to educate their daughters can send them to school, those who oppose it can keep them at home. It is the king's will, they are warned, that such schools are to go forth. Indeed, it so happens that there is another delegation from Buraida in town, they are told—one that came to press the case for girls' education. There are many in Buraida who don't want their town left out of the new blessings and largesse of the state.

It wasn't a straightforward affair, this battle. The chronicler of this struggle tells us that there were many who opposed girls' schooling in the daytime, and pressed for it under the cover of night. There were also noted men of means who had small private schools for their own daughters and relatives yet who opposed public schools for the education of others. The government alternated between laissez-faire and hard decisions that settled the recurring fights between the traditionalists and their rivals. Police protection was often needed for the new schools and their teachers, and the government provided it. The religious reactionaries fought these changes, then ended up sending their daughters to the very schools they had hitherto condemned. Purity gave in to self-interest. The bloggers and the pundits were having a field day with the handful of religious zealots who had spoken out against King Abdullah's big, new project. Soon, they prophesied, the daughters of the zealots would be bidding for admission to the prestigious new university. The state wields enormous power, its deference to the reactionaries is often a measure of its indifference to the sensibilities of the modernists. When challenged, the monarch had not blinked. Whether this university would have the "multiplier effect" its enthusiasts claimed for it is an altogether different endeavor. On the eastern edge of this vast country, there is another modern enclave, Aramco in Dhahran. It evokes small-town America in the early 1960s. It has decidedly "liberal" ways. But the world beyond its gates and checkpoints is not governed by Aramco's code.

There are (obvious) costs to rebellions, and (hidden, silent) costs to societies that opt for the stagnation of the status quo. Saudi Arabia was spared the damage of the so-called revolutions of the Arab and Islamic world. No colonels had risen at dawn and successfully seized the levers of power as the "Free Officers" had done in Egypt, Iraq, and Libya. No "armed imam" had stepped forth, as was the case in Iran, to impose a reign of virtue and terror. A middle class has been spawned by the oil wealth and the stability and by the spread of an educational system, but this class has never put in a bid for independent political power. There are currents borne by the wind which have given the House of Saud its primacy: the belief in conquest and in *ghazu'* (the raid) which endows the rule of the Sauds with legitimacy. In the desert fashion they had gone out and conquered the domain, and it is now theirs. The religious calling of the state was tethered to the power of kingly rule: the standing of the Wahhabi religious class and its authority have been a prop to the royal family. Arabia has been swept clean of other interpretations of Islam. The mystical Sufi tradition, long established in the Hijaz, has been overwhelmed; Shi'a communities in the Eastern Province and Ismailis (a small Shi'a sect) in the southwest survive, but they are on the defensive, and bereft of power and resources.

The most worldly part of the realm, the Hijaz—the center of the pilgrimage, at the crossroads of Muslims from as far away as North Africa, India, and Indonesia—has been reduced to subservience. The British-educated political writer Mai Yamani, herself a woman from the upper reaches of Hijazi society (her father, Ahmad Zaki Yamani, had risen to power and fame as oil minister in the 1970s and early 1980s, only to be later sidelined by King Fahd), has written of the erosion of Hijazi power. The very title of her major book, *Cradle of Islam: The Hijaz and the Quest for an Arabian Identity* (2004), tells of wounded pride and of the passing of a world. Oil income has been merciless: it functioned like a huge wrecking ball. Where pilgrimage had once been a source of considerable wealth, indeed accounting for three-fifths of the new Saudi state's revenues, oil income has dwarfed the wealth of the Hijazi merchants and notables.

Royal patronage has become a principal source of wealth. The House of Saud could now make or break fortunes. It could enrich Najdi men of business, it could make tycoons of outsiders like the Lebanese businessman Rafiq Hariri—outsiders content to live in the shadow of monarchy, marginal men happy to dwell on the wisdom and *asala* (authenticity) of the Sauds. Hijazis have been left with a stark choice: subservience to the rulers or a lapse into bitter nostalgia. Even the use of the name of the Hijaz has been discouraged—the proud urban centers of Jeddah, Mecca, Medina, and Taif now go by the name of the Western Province. It is inconceivable that a challenge to the realm could be mounted from the Hijaz. It would be sure to be overwhelmed by the material and cultural power of Najd. Hijazis in the know (Mai Yamani included) see the end of King Faisal's reign in 1975 as a turning point in their fortunes, for that monarch had been their patron, he had spent his formative years in their midst. His immediate successors—Khalid and Fahd—have not shared his affinity for the Hijaz and its people. More broadly, the loss of Hijazi influence is a product of the changes that have come to the country: the new, strict piety occasioned by the rise of Iran as a rival to Saudi Islam, the seizure of the Grand Mosque by the religious diehards, the price exacted by the Najdi religious class for its support of the monarchy. Najd and the House of Saud would chart their own way. Saudi Arabia would go on to accumulate new clout in the Arab-Islamic world, it would negotiate new terms of engagement with the world beyond. Gone was the edge of the worldly Hijazis.

The Hijazis were of course not alone in this sense of disinheritance in the face of Najdi power. In the southern hinterland, in the Province of Asir, this feeling of alienation runs deep, and we have seen it earlier in the autobiographical novel of Abdullah Thabit, *The 20th Terrorist*. The Islam of this hill country bore no resemblance to the austere Wahhabism of Najd, and there were sprinkled throughout the province offshoots of the Shi'a faith, Ismailis and Zaydis (another small Shi'a sect), heresies within heresies as the Wahhabi preachers and jurists would put it. "The southern part of Saudi Arabia has been kidnapped and held by a force of religious extremism," a man from Asir observed to me. "In less than thirty years it has been reshaped, a society that favored life and love and the song has been remade into a stern, unforgiving land."

The people in al-Hasa (renamed the Eastern Province since 1952) remain the quintessential stepchildren and outsiders of the realm. This coastal country in Eastern Arabia had been conquered in 1913, the first acquisition beyond Central Arabia of the emerging Saudi state. The Shi'a were a majority in Hasa, they were traders and cultivators, they carried on commerce with Bahrain and Basra, Oman and Bombay. They had deep reservoirs of water and date plantations. Ibn Saud was a practical man, he had struck here, Guido Steinberg writes in a perceptive essay, "The Shiites in the Eastern Province of Saudi Arabia, 1913–1953," because Najd could not produce "the necessary amount of foodstuff for all its inhabitants." Moreover, the trade routes from Southern Najd went through Hasa to Bahrain, across the Gulf. This population of Eastern Arabia, Steinberg adds, was to "bear the burden" of financing Ibn Saud's campaigns in Northern Najd, Hijaz, and Asir.

The "pacification" of this unhappy acquisition of the realm—pacification is the right term, I believe—was not a pretty tale. Wahhabi enforcers blew in with the conquest, there were *rafida* (rejecters of Islam), heretics in need of redemption, there were opportunities for extortion, the people of Hasa were to provide for the conquerors and religious enforcers. A cousin of Ibn Saud, cruel by the harshest standards of the desert, Abdullah bin Jaluwi, was sent there, the undisputed master of all around him, and his reign of terror smothered the independent life of the population. The town of Qatif, almost wholly Shi'a, had put up some resistance, but its scholars and urban notables were decimated: a good deal of their land was confiscated, the unyielding ones were executed or banished into exile. Fanatic Wahhabi warriors drawn from the Ikhwan, the Wahhabi shock troops, were unleashed on the Shi'a. The religious Shi'a ceremonies were banned, driven underground. Ibn Saud was at some remove from the place: he could unleash the official terror and then step in to soften the blows, he would give in to the Wahhabi *ulama* and then urge greater tolerance. It was hard work appeasing the Wahhabi preachers: they sought nothing less than the extirpation of Shi'ism.

Oil, and the wealth it brought in the aftermath of the Second World War, altered the life of the entire realm and the terms of engagement between the Saudi state and the Shi'a. The burden of taxation could be lifted, the zeal of the Wahhabi preachers and judges was checked. The great force in the land, the Arabian American Oil Company, gave new opportunities for the Shi'a, since the oil complex and the oil bounty were in their midst. An unsentimental realism had settled upon the Shi'a. Save for a maximalist or two who would speak of secession of this territory from the Saudi realm, they resigned themselves to their fate. The state and its ruling creed were not theirs, the Sauds could dispense a measure of mercy but not much more.

The protest that erupted in 1979—in the shadow of the Iranian Revolution—put on display the unhappiness of this population, and then its inability to throw off the Najdi dominion.

A thoughtful Shi'a intellectual from Qatif wrote to me in November 2009 about the unease of the Shi'a in the midst of a tangled fight on the Yemeni-Saudi border. "Our walls are probably higher than the Berlin Wall. The clashes with the Houthis in the south led many to question Saudi Shi'a loyalty to our country. We had to give a renewed declaration of loyalty, exactly as we did in all previous events where the Shi'a were involved, as you see, we are treated as members of a sect rather than citizens." The Houthis were Yemeni rebels, doctrinally they were Zaydis, an offshoot which by strict religious criteria is closer to the Sunnis than it is to the practice of Shi'ism. The Houthis were caught in a struggle against the secular autocracy of the Yemeni strongman, Ali Abdullah Salih: they sought autonomy in the northern part of their country. Their leader, Hussein Houthi, after whose tribe they are named, had fallen in battle in 2004, but the rebellion had persisted. The Yemeni strongman had pulled off a familiar political trick: the standoff with a band of rebels was turned into a proxy war between Iran and Saudi Arabia. The autocracy in Yemen knew no other trick. It needed Saudi patronage, and the clashes on the Yemeni-Saudi border were a natural concern of the Saudis. The rulers in Riyadh loathed the Houthis, and they had a congenital worry about the loyalty of the Ismailis and the Zaydis on their side of the border. No sooner had this Yemeni crisis begun to grow more deadly than the Wahhabi diehards stepped forth. In their eyes, the sins of the Houthis were the sins of the Shi'a everywhere—Iran and its tributaries in the Arab world.

The Shi'a intellectual who wrote to me of this new burden to his community was a man of his country, a reformer in the best sense of the term. But the culture of his country imposed its demands on him. It was in that spirit, and to ward off those charges of Shi'a disloyalty, that the leading Shi'a cleric in the Eastern Province, Shaykh Hassan al-Saffar, issued a statement of support of his country. "I can not help but stand by my nation against any violation to each span of its territories. . . . We are all partners in this nation and we must have a unified stand with the leadership against any aggression." Saffar called on Yemenis to "solve their problems inside their borders," and he had a plea to make, subtle but important in this climate, to the media and the writers in the Muslim world to refrain from "using sectarian language which harms the interest of the nation, especially in such sensitive circumstances. May Allah protect our country from all evil, and keep it safe from the intrigues of all aggressors."

I have met Shaykh Hassan al-Saffar, a man of deep culture and moderation. Months earlier, I called on him in a humble, small house that served as his office in Qatif. A trim, almost stylish man, born in 1958, he treated me to a simple lunch. He wore the tight-fitting tunic of a religious scholar and a white turban. The wire-rim glasses reflected the style of the man and his scholarly aura. We ate with plastic utensils, from paper plates, the meal the standard fare of salads and some chicken and cans of soda, brought in from a small establishment nearby. This was worlds removed from the palaces of the royals and from the glitter of Jeddah. The setting and the meal couldn't have been more spare, but the man himself was self-possessed and forthright and free of any dissimulation. He had behind him a life of political activism and opposition. He had known exile in Iran, Kuwait, and Syria. He had been something of a revolutionary in his youth, but he had made his peace with the rulers, reaching an accord with them back in 1993, when he returned to his homeland to work within the bounds of the political-religious order. More radical scholars and activists had seen that accord as a deed of surrender, but he would live with the choice he made. He had no aspiration to rule, no dreams of secession of the Eastern Province tugged at him. When I called on him, a more radical Shi'a scholar, Nimr al-Nimr, from a village on the outskirts of Qatif, had provoked a small storm by warning that the dignity of the Shi'a was more precious than the homeland and by speaking openly of the threat of secession. Shaykh Nimr was then a wanted man, he had gone underground, and young men stirred up by his passion had rallied to him, held vigil in front of his house. This was not Hassan al-Saffar's way. The Iranian religious utopia was not his, the passion of the Houthi gunmen was for this man an alien endeavor. He was in this country, but not fully of it. He would be called upon, time and again, to demonstrate his fealty to it.

The country, and its dominant religious creed, were what they were. A Shi'a cleric with social and political awareness had his work cut out for him. In the aftermath of the terror attacks in 2003 and 2004, and the scrutiny of the outside world, the custodians of power had signaled that they understood that all was not well in the realm and that religious extremism had to be reined in. But the religious class had its passions, and the powers that be in the political arena could not always control them.

There was something of a nonaggression pact between the dynasty and the religious class. So long as the preachers and the scholars acknowledged the primacy of the rulers, they were relatively free to indulge their passions and phobias. Much was made of the appointment to the Grand Mosque in Mecca of a black man, Shaykh Adel Kalbani. He was dubbed the Barack Obama of his religious guild; a racial barrier had fallen. But Kalbani soon provoked a storm in mid-2009, when he opined that the Shi'a religious scholars were heretics and apostates. Another scholar in Riyadh, Shaykh Mohamed Arifi, did him one better: he launched an attack against the most revered figure in the Shi'a religious constellation, Grand Ayatollah Ali Sistani, in Najaf, Iraq, branding that singularly moderate jurist heretical and corrupt. Yet another Wahhabi preacher decreed it impermissible, *haram*, to sell property to the Shi'a anywhere in the kingdom. This zeal was bottomless. It was impermissible, too, another man of the religious establishment advised, for a believer to visit his Shi'a neighbors or to return their greetings. The monarch could sponsor an "interfaith dialogue," he could journey to Madrid and New York, as he did, and convene international gatherings of religious figures from the world over. But the religious gatekeepers and enforcers had their deeply held beliefs about the ways of the faith. And the Shi'a religious scholars and lay activists were justified in their sense that the monarch had ventured abroad to mend fences with Jews and Christians while leaving the Sunni-Shi'a schism in his homeland to the mercy, and the agitation, of the Wahhabi extremists.

A worldly scholar of Hassan al-Saffar's sophistication and exposure to the modern media and the outside world was alert to his community's humiliations. He knew the ways of the Wahhabi establishment—the bigotry of the extremists within its ranks, the silence of others who quietly spoke of their unease with extremism but left the debate, and the new television channels and the pulpits, to the diehards. There was a contagious fever of extremism at play in the land, Saffar noted in a wide-ranging interview with the website of Al-Arabiya television in early January 2010. He was under no illusions about the balance of things in Saudi religious life. The Salafis (the fundamentalists, the religious reactionaries) had the upper hand, they had unlimited access to the media, they had the educational system and the judiciary, and precious few were willing to challenge the worldview they propagated. For their part, his Wahhabi rivals were secure that this land, the Arabian Peninsula, was theirs and theirs alone. Saffar could plead that the kind of sectarian bigotry loose in the land led to the estrangement of Saudi Arabia from the Shi'a in other Islamic countries, but this was a hollow threat: the Wahhabi establishment had no interest in an accommodation with other sects. It was one thing to step aside and let the monarch pursue a dialogue with Jews and Christians and Hindus, it was quite another to strike compromises with the *rafida*, the Shi'a heretics, over Islam itself.

In a penetrating and suggestive study of Castile in the mid-seventeenth century, historian J. H. Elliott described that Castilian world as a nonrevolutionary society. The material for revolt was in place, Castile had succumbed to a sense of defeat and disillusionment but was not overtaken by the revolutionary change that struck France and England. It fell back on its belief in kingship, the *poderosos* (the powerful ones, the oligarchical forces) threw their weight behind the monarchy. Elliott's narrative is remarkably close to the trajectory of Saudi history. Kingship rescued the Saudi world in the 1960s under Faisal, and gave it relief under Abdullah three decades later. Saudi Arabia would not pay the price of a generalized revolt. The militants of Al Qaeda could not win. The appeal of Osama bin Laden was never tested in the Saudi kingdom. He never came back from holy war abroad to summon the faithful at home. Would Najd have risen to his cause? There are grounds for skepticism as to the ability of that particular challenger to upend the monarchy. He was an outsider with a Yemeni father and a Syrian mother— and the descendant of a merchant—in a culture that gave honor to princes and to conquest.

In the absence of a generalized revolt that would impose a new social order, the realm is likely to muddle through. There will be bloggers pushing for reform, there will be modern, stylish women forced to step out into the public domain wrapped in their *abayas* and denied the right to a normal, whole life. Small changes will seem like large breakthroughs, a realm of this kind places severe limits on creativity. In 2005, there was an excited buzz in the country about a novel by a young Saudi woman, Rajaa Alsanea, *Girls of Riyadh*, which was released in Lebanon. The genre of the novel, in its modern form, had not been an Arabian one; poetry was the cultural medium of choice in this land. In any generous evaluation, this novel was a terrible literary disappointment. It yielded no insight into the society, it depicted the empty lives of a handful of wealthy young women. Its vindication lay in the act of its publication and no more. Its literary quality recalled the novels published in Cairo early in the twentieth century when modern fiction made its appearance in Egypt. Censorship and self-censorship limit what Saudis can say—and how far into the world they can see. In her author's note to the English translation of her novel, Rajaa Alsanea comes across as more the eager "ambassador" of her country than a writer challenging the codes of a restrictive culture.

> It never occurred to me when I wrote my novel, that I would be releasing it in any language other than Arabic. I did not think the Western world would actually be interested. It seemed to me, and to many other Saudis, that the Western world still perceives us either romantically, as the land of the Arabian Nights and the land where bearded sheikhs sit in their tents surrounded by their beautiful harem women, or politically, as the land that gave birth to Bin Laden and other terrorists, the land where women are dressed in black from head to toe and where every house has its own well in the backyard! Furthermore, coming from a family that values other cultures and nations, and being the proud Saudi I am, I felt it is my duty to reveal another side of Saudi life to the Western world. The task was not easy, however.

This was no heretical literary canon in the works. This was not an author who had come forth to challenge the verities of her world.

Countries have horizons—limits of the imagination, a sense of things that can and cannot be, imagined futures. Rulers and subjects and dissidents alike in this Saudi realm seem committed to the realm as it is—the rulers for the obvious advantages power grants them, the citizenry because they can't conceive how an order so intricate and entrenched could be taken apart and then put together again. The Saudi order could fend off the challenges—and the examples—of other lands. Across the border, there was the principality of Kuwait: women could drive, and vote, and run for the national parliament. There were several churches in Kuwait City where a variety of denominations could worship in broad daylight. In May 2009, several women contested the parliamentary election, and four of them—two Sunnis, two Shi'a—were elected to a parliament of fifty members. A barrier had been broken, this was the first time women had been elected to the national assembly. The four women were professionals of high educational accomplishment. The Islamists had agitated against the propriety and legitimacy of women running for the parliament. But Kuwaiti opinion was done with that prohibition. This was not a distant European example—it wasn't even Iraq, where women had a big role in the parliament—but a dynastic state nearby. Still, the Saudi system could take that Kuwaiti breakthrough in stride. The upholders of the Saudi order have never had a high opinion of parliaments and of open parliamentary debates where matters of state are laid bare. For the Saudi rulers and their allies in the religious establishment, Kuwait was a small principality, boisterous and given to political disputes, a land without the blessings and the limits imposed on a country that was home to Mecca and Medina. This Saudi realm of reserve and religious probity and caution—a prying, watchful society—would move at its own pace.

Under King Abdullah, Saudi political culture offered an Arabian version of the theme of the "good tsar" that ran through the life of the Russian autocracy. Intermittent, furious rebellions, peasant upheavals, punctuated Russian history as an expanding state herded its people into the modern world. As Paul Avrich aptly put it in a remarkable work, *Russian Rebels: 1600–1800*, ordinary Russians saw the state as a "giant octopus" which squeezed out their life's breath.

> Yet they always distinguished sharply between the tsar and his advisers. The tsar was their benevolent father, the bearer of justice and mercy, while the boyars were wicked usurpers, demons in human form who throve on the people's enslavement. To eliminate them—to "cleanse" or "remove" them from the land, as rebel propaganda put it—was their devout wish, for only by demolishing the wall of nobles and bureaucrats, they felt, could the ancient bond with the sovereign, on which their salvation depended, be restored.

In the reign of Abdullah the "good king," petitions and open letters were full of laments for what has befallen the realm: the obscurantism of the religious class, the plunder of public treasure, the impoverishment of broad segments of the population in a country awash with oil wealth, the growing power of the princes and their expanding and privileged role in the economic marketplace. In those appeals, the monarch is innocent of all these transgressions, a benevolent arbiter who would set things right if only he knew, if the sycophants and the palace guard and the vast royal household would let him in on the sordid workings of the realm.

In this vein, a surprisingly brave and quite sweeping indictment of the state of public affairs was addressed to the monarch by a prominent public figure in early 2010, one Dr. Abdullah al-Hamed, who identifies himself as a member of the "society for civil and political rights in the Kingdom of Saudi Arabia." An exhaustive autopsy that ran well over a dozen pages and was widely circulated through the internet, the petition was prompted by heavy rains which fell on Jeddah in late November 2009. The rain exposed Jeddah's inadequate sewage system. A large metropolitan area, the kingdom's commercial capital, lacked a decent treatment facility for its sewage. Massive flooding may have caused the deaths of five hundred people; entire neighborhoods were overwhelmed by the floods. The municipality had been unable to cope with the disaster. Jeddah's ordeal (like that of New Orleans during Hurricane Katrina) became a statement on the shortcomings of the public order and on the gap between the wealth of the realm and the inadequacy of its services.

From the debacle that befell Jeddah, Abdullah al-Hamed ranged far and wide. The "Jeddah calamity," he wrote, "should have sounded the alarm to awaken us in our country, where the life of the citizen is cheap indeed, and where people were left by the authorities to be swept by floods and the sewers even though billions of dollars were marked for contracts and public works that have never been carried out." The "princes of darkness" and their cabals of thieves had made off with public money, their theft aided by the absence of a free press that could have taken up the question of corruption. A commission had been established, this petitioner wrote, to combat corruption and to advance the cause of transparency, but it had died in infancy, and nothing came of it. The "culture of corruption" had taken root in the country, the "mafias" had proliferated, all protected by members of the royal household, princes with absolute power, exempt from scrutiny and accountability. The princes, Dr. al-Hamed reminded the monarch, have tightened their grip on the public life. They now run the provinces of the country, they have claimed for themselves domains in municipal affairs and environmental protection and the like that had been the preserve of commoners. And where commoners are left at the head of institutions and ministries, they are "front men" for the real powers—the royals. There had been a tacit agreement in the realm: power to the princes, commerce to the merchants. This division of roles, Abdullah al-Hamed wrote, has been shredded. The princes are now active in schemes large and small: they own restaurant chains, taxi concessions, they are land speculators, they help themselves to lucrative oil deals which enable them to sell oil off the books in world markets. The "second generation" of princes has become particularly good at coming up with schemes for quick enrichment, costly contracts are given to them, while the living standard of the Saudi population at large erodes by the day. In neighboring oil lands, hundreds of billions of dollars have been set up for future generations, but the Saudi realm lacks this protection. A mere 22 percent of Saudis own their homes, the rest are tenants, in a country where oil ought to be the patrimony of all citizens.

This petitioner was unsparing, and was writing of things that were the stuff of gossip—and public knowledge: the land grants given to the royals, the confiscation of public land for private development by the more powerful of the princes, the absentee governors of the provinces who live abroad and return only when there are deals to be made. No one cries "halt" to this abuse; the editors of the major dailies are appointed by the powers that be, not to mention the ownership by the princes and their in-laws of "empires of information," television channels, newspapers, that glorify the achievements of the "inspired princes" who own these means of communication. "Yes, Custodian of the Two Holy Mosques, you have issued many reform decrees, but they have not been carried out. The citizenry have lost all hope, there is rampant unemployment among the men and women, but the princes and their courtiers continue to import foreign laborers on whom they impose monthly kickbacks reminiscent of the slavery of bygone age," al-Hamed wrote. Nothing escaped the net of these princes: a ban some years back on the import of satellite dishes created a black market for that coveted item, and the beneficiaries made fortunes in the process. An open parliamentary life might have exposed the abuse, but silence engulfs the country. It is a petitioner's trick: the "good king" knows of the abuse and doesn't, he stands outside the circle of the accused, but that circle is perilously close to him. The structures of oppression and plunder are not quite his, but they answer to him, the beneficiaries are his countless nephews, present everywhere. The "good king," particularly one so advanced in age, is both a repository of hope and a way of dodging the difficulty of repairing entrenched structures of order.

A perfect storm hit the world economy in late 2008. This, too, in an odd way, served the purposes of the custodians of the Saudi order. To be sure, the Saudis could not emerge unscathed as oil rose to $140 a barrel in mid-2008 before it collapsed to

$40 a barrel by the end of the year. The storm touched them, but lightly when compared to the damage that befell economies the world over. International banks pulled back from corporate financing, but Saudi banks were on the whole well capitalized, they had not trusted the new financial instruments. There were no credit default swaps in Riyadh and no populist pressures on Saudi banks to grant loans to those who could not afford to pay them back; their mortgages were not "securitized." The financial sector did not bulk as large in the Saudi economy as it did in the United States, the European Union, and the other Arab states of the Persian Gulf. As percentage of GDP, the Saudi financial market stood at 75 percent, compared to 97 percent in the United States, 112 percent in the European Union, and an average 104 percent in the other Arab states of the Gulf. In a financial calamity that hit equities without mercy, the Saudi foreign assets were heavily invested in U.S. Treasuries. Caution had shown up the new financial instruments and their creators.

For more than a decade, the Saudis had had a case of Dubai envy and resentment. There was "buzz" about Dubai and swagger. The foreign press was smitten with the city-state, its ruler Mohamed bin Rashed had become something of an international celebrity, he had reinvented a place of little consequence and endowment into a hub of commerce, finance, and tourism. The expats loved Dubai and its extravagance—the Dubai World Cup, the world's richest horse race, had become an event of note on the calendar of the well-heeled; real estate speculation knew no restraint. But the boom had been built on debt, and the economy of Dubai had gone bust. Hundreds of cranes and dredgers ground to a halt. Those pundits and outsiders smitten with Dubai had moved on. Countless expats deserted the place. The Saudis had felt vindicated by the stumble of Dubai. They were not given to this kind of exuberance, their restricted mores would not permit the night life and liberties of Dubai. They had opted for a safer course, they had avoided the speculative investment in real estate that had become the norm in Dubai and other Arab states of the Gulf, and could feel that they had been good stewards of the oil windfall that came their way in the 2003–8 years.

"We have seen wealth come and go, and come back again," a young businessman with an American education and an international reach said to me.

> But some of our fundamental problems persist. We still can't get good schooling for our children, and those of us who can afford it send them abroad. We are supposed to hire Saudis, but we don't have the right kind of Saudis to hire. When we give them jobs, they turn up and idle the time on their mobiles talking to their friends—the work is done by Pakistanis and Bangladeshis. We have not undertaken the reforms we need, our wealth hides our troubles. We have a good and decent king, but beneath the level of kingship, the old ways prevail.

There are highly motivated individuals within the system, younger men in their thirties and forties, they mean well, a peer of his, a policy analyst for the government, added. But the bureaucracy, awesome in size and now deeply entrenched, stifles them. They can't turn things around with the ease that an earlier generation of technocrats, starting from scratch, had been able to do.

The outside world comes to Saudi Arabia, but largely on Saudi terms. Former American officials (even a former president or two) in search of deals and speaking fees are commonplace in Jeddah and Riyadh: they say little about the internal practices of Saudi Arabia, and know little about them. The economic pressures weigh heavily on the industrial democracies and their leaders: when those leaders turn up in Arabia, they do so for big economic projects and contracts vital to their workers and corporations at home. Saudi self-confidence has grown with the years. China has risen, and its model of economic openness and political autocracy is congenial to the Saudis. As more Saudi oil was finding its way to China, India, and Far Eastern markets, the Saudi sensitivity to the norms of the democracies, never particularly strong to begin with, has eroded. The Chinese come for commerce, and nothing else, they want secure oil supplies and deeper inroads into a lucrative Saudi market. They have nothing to say about the internal order of the Saudi state. Indeed, they themselves are as compulsive as the Saudis about warding off outside intervention in their affairs.

The Saudis are quite assertive about the uniqueness of their world, their land being the birthplace of Islam, home to Mecca and Medina. In the scheme of things, they have laid claim to a heavy dosage of cultural autonomy, declaring outsiders largely unfit to judge them. For better or worse, the Saudis are on their own, their world what they make of it themselves. This truism breaks down when the Saudis venture abroad, when their charities and their preachers, and their young, pitiless jihadists, and their well-financed media intrude on other lands, denying those lands the tranquility the Saudis crave for themselves.

In a world where Saudis stay at home, their educational curriculum would only be a concern for the students taking in that knowledge, and the parents weighing the merits of what truths are transmitted to their children. But the outside world is perfectly entitled to judge the Saudi worldview when young men forged in that culture take what they have been given and taught, carry their wrath and their dread of "the other" beyond Saudi borders.

The ethos of the Arabian Peninsula's cultural uniqueness can become an all-too-convenient alibi for intolerance and self-righteousness. There can only be one true faith in Arabia and one true doctrine of that faith (the Wahhabi creed) while other countries, "normal" lands, can be judged by one and all. Thus a country that denies the Shi'a minority in the Eastern Province access to the military and to diplomatic posts, and to the full sense of citizenship and belonging, can grant itself the right to sit in judgment on the way Iraq negotiates its way out of the sectarian impasse between the Sunni rulers of the past and the new order that gave the Shi'a of that country political primacy. In the same vein, the irony is lost on a Saudi political and religious class that agitated against a Swiss vote which rejected the construction of new minarets in Switzerland as it overlooked the draconian limits and restrictions on any form of non-Islamic practice in the kingdom. The Sunni clerics calling for an economic boycott of Switzerland, in the aftermath of that country's decisive vote against new minarets, on November 29, 2009, couldn't comprehend the great irony of their passion. They were demanding of the Swiss tolerance they haven't asked of themselves. In their view of things, their country's uniqueness acquitted it of the burden of reciprocal tolerance. The kingdom, observed one religious figure, the *imam* of the Grand Mosque in Mecca, was the *qibla* of Muslims everywhere (the direction of the Kaaba in Mecca toward which Muslims must turn during prayers). Thus "not a single church bell will ring in the Saudi territory." The world may wink at this lack of reciprocity, but damage is incurred by a people who grant themselves that kind of absolution from reciprocal norms.

The regime had answered the military challenge of Al Qaeda, and—no surprise—its "rifle and sword" had prevailed. In mid-2009, in a long-awaited trial of nearly a thousand militants, the criminal courts handed out prison sentences to 330 and sentenced one Al Qaeda leader to death. A discerning observer of his country said that all that was "surgery" when the skill his country needed was knowledge and treatment of "viruses." The virus of religious radicalism and of intolerance had not been treated, he added. The Ministry of Interior and the police can't cope with the malady. The order lacked the skill—and the candor—to face that deeper challenge. He was of this order, he said, he was loyal to his country, he had no patience or sympathy for any schemes of revolt. He thought that the rulers were too clever by half, that they exaggerated their ability to control the forces of religious reaction that they had indulged. For now, the rulers had the upper hand, he conceded, but he warned that the zealots were winning in the countryside, in the rural hamlets, and among the urban poor. He saw the religious reactionaries as a cunning, patient lot. They wait, secure in the belief that their worldview is seeping into the land.

"The rulers wink at all this at their own peril," he added:

Yes, the rulers have the money and the bureaucratic apparatus and the big palaces, but the religious class has the people
all to itself. The preachers can summon the people to the
causes that stir them, appeal to their passions. We could have
had a secular state had we followed in the footsteps of Ibn
Saud. But his sons were lesser men, they gave in, the extremists have had their way for a long time now, and there is no
way of knowing how this will end. The future of the country
is one big unknown. There is a silent crisis in the land, the
bombs are not going off, Saudis are not out in open rebellion.
But the silent crisis—the young men who can't marry, who
can't find employment or adequate housing, who have nothing to look forward to—stalks us all, rulers and ruled alike.

The hold of the royals on the country remains quite
extraordinary. Saudis—some of them quoted in this text—
speak of an increasingly younger country outgrowing the writ
of the Sauds. Of this, I remain skeptical. The "opening" of
Arabia in recent years bears the mark of the man at the helm,
King Abdullah. Perhaps the man was merely an instrument
of wider forces at work, a leader who caught a ride on a
societal wave of change. Things were changing in the country—
the spread of education, the scrutiny of the outside world,
the recognition by growing numbers of Saudis that religious
radicalism and unchecked zeal had led them and their country
to a blind alley—and a shrewd political guardian had sensed
that "reform" was the safer course for his realm and his family's
inheritance. The Sauds had been good at assigning different roles
to different princes; thus has the dynasty survived and prospered.
Doubtless, Abdullah had the writ of the senior princes for the

course he embarked upon. The talk of dissatisfaction on the part of this or that half-brother of his was the steady gossip that surrounds this secretive royal house.

But the personal factor matters in a monarchy of this sort. And herein lies the question that can only be a matter of conjecture: what becomes of this reformist impulse when Abdullah passes from the scene? Desert chronicles are not particularly reliable, but the best guess for King Abdullah's year of birth is 1923. As of this writing, in 2010, the Saudi ruler was in his late eighties. His Crown Prince, his half-brother, Sultan, was only a year younger, and ailing. This Saudi dominion has survived many obituaries of its imminent demise. Younger inheritors will step forth, and they will make their preferences felt as to the balance between authority and needed change. But a process of reform so closely tied to the preferences of an old ruler was one that rendered the more enlightened in Saudi Arabia nervous about the staying power of the changes that have come their way in recent years. What one prince grants, another might be tempted to take back.

CHAPTER FIVE

Coda:
In the Time of the Americans

When a young mining engineer by the name of Thomas Barger, Minnesota born but raised and educated in North Dakota, arrived in Arabia in 1937, in Dhahran to be exact, it was, of course, a simpler age. It was then that the "modern" Arabian world was "invented," and the solitude and the poverty of the desert world were both disturbed and ameliorated by new means and possibilities. It was the Great Depression at home; Barger, twenty-nine years of age, was madly in love with Kathleen Ray, a young rancher's daughter from Medora, North Dakota. The work of a mining engineer was hard to find; he had worked as a miner to make ends meet. An offer came from Standard Oil of California to go prospecting for oil in Arabia and to do geological surveys. He took it and went to Arabia without his bride.

It would be several years before she could join him. He was to know adventure and to rise to the rank of chief executive officer of Aramco, the Arabian American Oil Company, and chairman of its board. He and this band of pioneers would bring forth a whole new world. A steady stream of letters he sent to his young bride back in North Dakota catches the wonder of that encounter in its early years of innocence. (The letters have been assembled and superbly edited by the Bargers' son, Timothy. The Bargers would have six children in Arabia; by a twist of fate, I would teach one of their daughters, Norah, at Princeton. I could not have known then what yearning and adventure went into her parents' life.) Here is Tom Barger on January 19, 1938, rendering to Kathleen, back on the ranch in North Dakota, the simplicity of the world he had ventured into:

> January 19, 1938
> Jabal Dhahran
> The soldiers are curious about everything. When Walt told them about winter in America, they couldn't understand why anyone would live in a country piled in ice and snow half of the year. Often when he tells them something particularly astounding, especially if it is man-made, one of them, usually old Salih, will say, "*Allah Akbar*," God is the greatest. The others follow suit and say, "*Allah Akbar*," presumably to show that after all it doesn't amount to much. . . . These poor people have no doctors and only the simplest and crudest of remedies. Despite their "*Enshallah*," if God wills, they are desperately eager to be doctored. A geologist out here has to be an amateur physician.

And from a letter dated February 20, 1938:

> Jerry and I spent the night swapping stories with the soldiers around the campfire. Jerry told about Daniel Boone throwing tobacco in the eyes of his Indian captors and swinging over a river gorge on a vine to make his escape. I stumbled through Custer's Last Stand. The Indians are

called the "American Bedu" and the soldiers, "the Army of the Government." Khamis and the rest are used to my terminology and especially love the Indian names such as Crazy Horse, Red Cloud and Rain in the Face.

Abdul Hadi hadn't heard of the Indians before and was fascinated by them. He wanted to know where they lived and finally ventured his opinion that they must be related to the tribes in Iraq. Salim Abu Ar-Ru'us doesn't take much interest in our stories because he can't understand our Arabic, so he sits crooning softly to himself. This can be disconcerting to the storyteller, but is apparently good Arabian etiquette.

Men did not know each other then, but there was less rancor. It hadn't been perfect harmony then. A young Wahhabi cleric, who would come into great authority in the years to come, one Abdulaziz ibn Baz, was heard from in 1939 lamenting that Ibn Saud had sold the land to the unbelievers. There is no need to prettify that desert world, and Barger didn't. I hazard to guess that his Saudi counterparts and men and women of his and his wife's age didn't either.

There is a memory older still than the time of Dhahran and the American oil prospectors, a time when America, in the Arabian Peninsula, was only the story of a distant land and of a benevolent leader. It was 1922: a visitor from the Levant, Ameen Rihani, a Christian Lebanese author who would fall under the spell of Ibn Saud, had come to the desert to meet the rising Arabian chieftain. Rihani knew the outside world, and Ibn Saud was curious to know about the "fall" of President Woodrow Wilson. It was hard for the desert ruler to understand how the Americans chose their leaders. Rihani had sketched for him the basics of the American way: parties, elections. "Strange! And does it not lead them to war?" the ruler asked. "What of Wilson?" he added. He was gone "because the majority was not with him in the last elections," his visitor replied. (Wilson had of course served two terms and had left office an ailing, broken man. But such was the answer Rihani had given Ibn Saud.)

"I do not think they did well," Ibn Saud observed of the American electorate. "Wilson is a great man. And his is the credit for awakening the small oppressed nations of the world. Wilson showed them the way to freedom and independence. He has infused, especially into the people of the East, a new spirit. He has also made America known to us. . . . America is the mother of all weak nations, and we Arabs are of them. . . . I liken Europe today to a great iron door, but there is nothing behind it."

It was easier then between nations—before the resentful dependence and the entanglements. This was a good generation before Thomas Barger and the other American prospectors and oilmen ventured into the Peninsula, forever altering its rhythm and its ways.

Source Notes

This work has been several years in the making. It is informed, in the background, by repeated visits to Saudi Arabia in the 1990s. More directly, in this writing I drew on the field notes of three visits that I made in 2002, then 2009.

I read the Saudi press on a consistent basis. The press is both censored and self-censored. Still, it provides a window onto the worldview of the rulers and their allies in the religious establishment. By Saudi standards, the press has grown braver and more open in recent years. There is more daring in taking on social and cultural issues than matters of high politics. Three daily newspapers were helpful to me. *Al-Watan*, a fairly liberal organ, owned and sponsored by a member of the royal clan, has been the most daring in the face of the conservative religious establishment. Two offshore papers also owned by members of the House of Saud are steady readings of mine, *Al Hayat* and *Asharq Al-Awsat*, both published in London. Of late, the bloggers have turned up in Arabia; this "cyber resistance," tailor-made for a country not given to words and open dissent, has been illuminating. Two sites, *Saudi Jeans* and *Saudiwave*, have been quite helpful. There is an electronic liberal magazine,

Elaph, which is unique and indispensable in the current Arab landscape, and I have repeatedly turned to it.

The fax reigned supreme when the "road to dissension" opened in Arabia in the 1990s. A huge volume of faxes and leaflets and petitions cluttered the machines; I accumulated them and drew on them. An enterprising scholar, Joshua Teitelbaum, wrote a fully documented and considered monograph on that turn in Saudi religious and political life, *Holier Than Thou: Saudi Arabia's Islamic Opposition* (Washington, D.C.: The Washington Institute for Near East Policy, 2000). The Egyptian American scholar Mamoun Fandy sketched this period at some length in his book *Saudi Arabia and the Politics of Dissent* (London: Palgrave Macmillan, 1999).

An admiring author, Mahmoud al-Rifaii, wrote the story of the most prominent of the religious diehards of the 1990s in a book (in Arabic) whose title translates to *The Reformist Project in Saudi Arabia,* published in 1995, no publisher or place of publication indicated. This book is useful for all the petitions and leaflets that were a standard feature of that phase. In an earlier study, I covered this period of disputation and provided a translation of some of this literature and pamphleteering, "Shooting an Elephant: The Expedition and Its Aftermath," in Joseph Nye and Roger Smith, editors, *After the Storm: Lessons from the Gulf War* (Lanham, Maryland: Madison Books, 1992), pp. 113–44.

The seizure of the Grand Mosque in Mecca in 1979—a signal event in recent Saudi history—has been extensively analyzed and described. Yaroslav Trofimov's *The Siege of Mecca* (New York: Doubleday, 2007) is the most accessible account. Joseph Kechichian's "Islamic Revivalism and Change in Saudi Arabia: Juhayman al-Utaybi's letters to the Saudi People," *The Muslim World*, January 1990, pp. 1–16, is particularly illuminating for the worldview of the leader of this rebellion. The traditional doctrine of Wahhabism, and the bargain between the rulers and the religious class, has a truly fine treatment in Christine Moss Helms, *The Cohesion of Saudi Arabia* (Baltimore: Johns Hopkins University Press, 1981).

Abdullah Thabit's unique autobiographical novel *The 20th Terrorist (Al-Irhabi 20)* was published in Damascus (Al Mada Publishers, 2006). An experienced, tenacious journalist, Faiza Ambah, was the first to write of this novel in the American press in her dispatch, "The Would-Be Terrorist's Explosive Tell-All Tale," *The Washington Post*, July 26, 2006.

Matthew Levitt and Michael Jacobson covered the issue of terrorist financing in their monograph, *The Money Trail: Finding, Following, and Freezing Terrorist Finances* (Washington, D.C.: The Washington Institute for Near East Policy, November 1, 2008). Oxford Analytica in 2009 had a brief report, "International Focus to Remain on Terrorist Financing." The Government Accountability Office's report, "U.S.–Saudi Counterterrorism Efforts," 2009, takes up the question of financial support, and the measures undertaken to cut off support for radical causes. U.S. Treasury Department under secretary Stuart Levey has been for several years the American official with the deepest knowledge of the financing of terrorism. His remarks on the money trail in Saudi Arabia quoted in the text can be found in the monograph by Levitt and Jacobson.

Bob Woodward's "first draft" of the history of the George W. Bush presidency has a convincing portrait of the evolution in Saudi thinking on Iraq. See *Plan of Attack*, published in 2004, and *The War Within*, published in 2008 (both New York: Simon & Schuster).

A trove of documents captured in Iraq by American forces—the so-called Sinjar Records—are a unique source of information about Saudis and other fighters who made their way to Iraq to wage a ferocious campaign of terrorism against the Iraqis and the Americans. Joseph Felter and Brian Fishman, of the Combating Terrorism Center at the U.S. Military Academy in West Point, New York, have a good summary of the data in their report "Al Qaeda's Foreign Fighters in Iraq," published by the Center in 2008. I went through the raw data for the backgrounds of the Saudi fighters, the money they brought with them, their route of entry, etc. The data was made available in 2007.

King Abdullah's remarks to the American diplomat Dennis Ross came from an account in the *New York Times Magazine* (August 2, 2009, "The Making of an Iran Policy," Roger Cohen).

The Institute for International Finance's "GCC Regional Overview," September 28, 2009, provided a good summation of the economies of Saudi Arabia and the smaller states of the Gulf in the aftermath of the global economic crisis of 2008. Samba Financial Group in Riyadh provides quite thorough analyses in its Report Series of the Saudi economy. I relied on its "Saudi Arabia: 2009 Mid-Year Economic Review and Forecast," published in June 2009.

On the question of the Shi'a in the Eastern Province, I had my field notes, and I read closely the following sources, several first-rate studies: Toby Jones, "Embattled in Arabia; Shi'is and the Politics of Confrontation in Saudi Arabia," Occasional Paper Series, Combating Terrorism Center at West Point, June 2009; Toby Mattheisen, "The Shi'a of Saudi Arabia at a Crossroads," *Middle East Report Online*, May 6, 2009. Particularly rich and insightful was Guido Steinberg's study "The Shiites in the Eastern Province of Saudi Arabia, 1913–1953," in Rainer Brunner and Werner Ende, editors, *The Twelver Shia in Modern Times* (Leiden, the Netherlands: Brill, 2001). There is an invaluable first-person account by the Shi'a writer and activist Fouad Ibrahim, *The Shi'is of Saudi Arabia* (London: Saqi Books, 2006). The unrest in the Eastern Province in 1979 is the subject of a first-rate essay by Toby Jones, "Rebellion on the Saudi Periphery: Modernity, Marginalization, and the Shia Uprising of 1979," *International Journal of Middle East Studies*, vol. 38, 2006, pp. 213–3.

The place of the Hijaz and its people in the new Najdi-dominated order is taken up by the Hijaz-born writer Mai Yamani in her book *Cradle of Islam: The Hijaz and the Quest for an Arabian Identity* (London: I. B. Tauris, 2004). Rajaa Alsanea's *Girls of Riyadh* is a stab at feminist literature, and an example of its limitations (New York: Penguin Press, 2007). I drew on a first-rate account (in Arabic) of the education of women in Saudi Arabia, which translates as *The Sedition of the Education of Girls*, by Abdullah al-Washmi, published in Casablanca in 2009 by the Arab Cultural Center.

On the question of women and their education, John Stuart Mill's "The Subjection of Women," written in 1869, can be found in J. S. Mill, *On Liberty and Other Writings* (Cambridge, England: Cambridge University Press, 1989), pp. 119–217. Joshua Muravchik has an illuminating portrait of the Saudi feminist Wajeha al-Huwaider in his book *The Next Founders: Voices of Democracy in the Middle East* (New York and London: Encounter Books, 2009), pp. 10–44.

Turki al-Hamad is a prolific, American-educated author and political writer whose work I have turned to and drawn on in this text. His "coming of age" autobiographical works, *Adama* and *Shumaisi*, published, respectively, in 2003 and 2005, were issued in London by Saqi Books. Also illuminating is his novel *The Wind of Paradise* (London: Saqi Books, 2005), an attempt to render, in fiction, the young terrorists who pulled off the attacks of 9/11, and the wider culture that produced them.

The Princeton scholar Michael Cook's majestic work *Commanding Right and Forbidding Wrong in Islamic Thought*

(Cambridge, England, and New York: Cambridge University Press, 2001) explains the philosophical underpinnings of Wahhabism and the manner in which the zeal at home became a substitute for expansion beyond the borders of the Saudi realm.

While reflecting on the ways of Saudi politics, I found a useful precedent in the historical patterns of Spanish—particularly Castilian—history. My remarks on Spain are drawn from the distinguished historian J. H. Elliott, particularly his book *Spain, Europe, and the Wider World* (New Haven and London: Yale University Press, 2009). The theme of the "good tsar" can be found in Paul Avrich, *Russian Rebels: 1600–1800* (New York and London: W. W. Norton, 1976).

The "time of the Americans" in Arabia has been endlessly recalled and written about. One readable narrative that covers the encounter between the American pioneers and Arabia is Anthony Cave Brown, *Oil, God, and Gold: The Story of Aramco and the Saudi Kings* (Boston: Houghton Mifflin, 1999). Thomas Barger's *Out in the Blue, Letters from Arabia, 1937–1940* (Vista, California: Selwa Press, 2000) is, as my text makes clear, a son's tribute to the wonder of the world that his parents found when the Americans first ventured into the Arabian Peninsula. Ameen Rihani is the Lebanese author cited in the text who came under the spell of Ibn Saud and gave him an account of Woodrow Wilson's political fate, *Ibn Saud of Arabia* (London: Constable, 1928).

No author can escape the spell of the "classics" of travel literature on Arabia. William Gifford Palgrave's *Personal Narrative of a Year's Journey through Central and Eastern Arabia 1862–1863* (London: Macmillan, 1868) is timeless. David Hogarth's *The Penetration of Arabia* (New York: Frederick A. Stokes, 1904) is a book of real insight and beauty. The best such chronicle is Charles Doughty's *Travels in Arabia Deserta* (London: Jonathan Cape, 1926).

About the Author

Fouad Ajami (1945–2014) was a Lebanese-born American scholar and writer. He taught first at Princeton University and then, for thirty years, was director of Middle East Studies at Johns Hopkins School of Advanced International Studies. He wrote and spoke extensively on Middle Eastern issues over the course of nearly forty years. He was the Herbert and Jane Dwight Senior Fellow at the Hoover Institution, Stanford University, and the cochair of its Herbert and Jane Dwight Working Group on Islamism and the International Order. He wrote numerous books, including *The Arab Predicament, Beirut: City of Regrets, The Vanished Imam: Musa al-Sadr and the Shia of Lebanon, The Dream Palace of the Arabs, The Foreigner's Gift: The Americans, the Arabs, and the Iraqis in Iraq, The Syrian Rebellion, In This Arab Time*, and a monograph, *The Struggle for Mastery in the Fertile Crescent*. His writings also include more than four hundred essays on Arab and Islamic politics, U.S. foreign policy, and contemporary international history. Ajami received numerous awards, including the MacArthur Fellows Award (1982) and the National Humanities Medal. His writings charted the road to 9/11, the Iraq War, and the U.S. presence in the Arab-Islamic world.

Iraq after America: Strongmen, Sectarians, Resistance
Joel Rayburn

In This Arab Time: The Pursuit of Deliverance
Fouad Ajami

America and the Future of War: The Past as Prologue
Williamson Murray

Israel Facing a New Middle East:
In Search of a National Security Strategy
Itamar Rabinovich and Itai Brun

Russia and Its Islamic World: From the Mongol
Conquest to the Syrian Military Intervention
Robert Service

Revolution and Aftermath:
Forging a New Strategy Toward Iran
Eric Edelman and Ray Takeyh

ESSAY SERIES

THE GREAT UNRAVELING: THE REMAKING OF THE MIDDLE EAST
In Retreat: America's Withdrawal from the Middle East
Russell A. Berman

Israel and the Arab Turmoil
Itamar Rabinovich

Reflections on the Revolution in Egypt
Samuel Tadros

The Struggle for Mastery in the Fertile Crescent
Fouad Ajami

The Weaver's Lost Art
Charles Hill

The Consequences of Syria
Lee Smith

Essays

Saudi Arabia and the New Strategic Landscape
Joshua Teitelbaum

Islamism and the Future of the Christians of the Middle East
Habib C. Malik

Syria through Jihadist Eyes: A Perfect Enemy
Nibras Kazimi

The Ideological Struggle for Pakistan
Ziad Haider

Syria, Iran, and Hezbollah:
The Unholy Alliance and Its War on Lebanon
Marius Deeb

The Story of the Tunisian Revolution
Samuel Tadros

Strategic Planning for the New Administration
Colin Dueck

What Is at Stake in Yemen
Fahad Nazer

From the Iranian Corridor to the Shia Crescent
Fabrice Balanche

Reflections on the Revolution in Egypt
Samuel Tadros

Index

U.S. presidential elections and,
122–23
See also specific monarch/prince
Houthi, Hussein, 168
Houthis, 168
al-Humayyin, Abdulaziz, 143
Hussein, Imam, 42
Hussein, Saddam, 25, 110
al-Huwaider, Wajeha, 154

ibn Abdul Wahhab, Muhammad,
xvii–xviii
ibn Abdulaziz, Prince Naif
as autocrat, 4
character of, 3–4
Committee for the Promotion
of Virtue and, 149–50
denial of, 63–64
King Abdullah's raising of, 3
Riyadh bombings and, 96
ibn Abdulaziz, Prince Talal
Free Princes and, 62
on reform, 17
ibn Bayyan, Hayyan
background on, 15
compromise of, 15–16
open letter by, 15
Ibn Baz, Abdulaziz, 52, 189
al-Awda and, 53–54
booklet issued by, 35–36
death of, 59
Dhahran attack response
by, 37
al-Hawali and, 49, 53–54

memorandum of advice and,
31, 32–33
ibn Jibrin, Abdullahi, 52
Riyadh bombings and, 81
Ibn Saad al-Qahtani, Muhammad,
50
Ibn Saud, Abd al-Aziz
America and, 120
background of, 42–43
British and, 43–44, 120
Hasa and, 166–67
Ikhwan and, 43–44
Rihani and, 189–90
Sibila, battle of, and, 44
sons of, 16–18
al-Utaybi and, 45
women's education and, 162
al-ikhtilat (mixing of men/
women), 151
Ikhwan ("the brothers," a religio-
tribal corps)
background of, 43
defeat of, 44
Ibn Saud reining in, 43–44
al-Utaybi and, 44–45
imara (principality), 66
"Impediments to Jihad"
(Zawahiri), 105
intiharis (suicidals), 111
Iran
Bush administration and,
124
election in, 125
Iraqi Shi'a and, 109–10

Shi'a political development analyst
  author's first impressions of, 6–7
  background of, 7
  on basic rights, 8–9
  on freedom, 9
  on oppression, 8
  on political parties/reforms, 8
"Shiites in the Eastern Province
    of Saudi Arabia, The"
    (Steinberg), 166
Shultz, George, 126
Shuyukh al-Sahwa (Shaykhs of the
    Awakening), 51
Sibila, battle of, 44
sira (conduct), 82
Sistani, Ali, 171
sleeper cells, 96
sorcery, 149
"splendid isolation," 36
Steinberg, Guido, 166
Subjection of Women, The (Mill), 153
Sudais, Abdulrahman
  on foreign travel/tourism, 72
  on Jews, 73
suicide bombings
  support for, 95
  Yemen and, 23
Sultan, Crown Prince
  future and, 186
  al-thaluth and, 4
sunna (conduct), 68
Sunnis
  Bahrain and, 131
  Hariri, Rafiq, and, 128–29
  Iraq war and, 107, 127

Lebanon and, 127–28, 129
  pact regarding, 130
Switzerland, 183
Syria
  healing rift with, 133–34
  issues in dealing with, 132
  Lebanese relations with,
    133–35
  revolutionary upheaval in, xxiv
Syrian contractors, 111–12

Taif, 21
takfir (declaring others
    apostates), 103
Talal, Prince. *See* ibn Abdulaziz,
    Prince Talal
Taliban, financing of, 135–36
Talibanization, 92
tauhid (assertion of divine unity
    of God), xviii
television
  Al-Arabiya, 123
  al-Awda and, 5
  cinema and, 139
  al-Qarni and, 5, 68
Terror Cell Member confessions,
    101–4
  Number 28, 104
  Number 27, 104
  Numbers 11, 12, and 26, 103
  Numbers 1 and 3, 102–3
terrorism
  Afghan-Pakistani theater and,
    135–36
  financing of, 122, 135–36